Vision Statement

Stone Lakes National Wildlife Refuge belongs to a limited group among the 540 national wildlife refuges that protect fish, wildlife, and habitat within an urban area. Through collaboration with public and private partners, Stone Lakes conserves and enhances a range of scarce Sacramento-San Joaquin Delta and Central Valley habitats and the fish, wildlife, and plants they support. It sustains freshwater wetlands, wooded riparian corridors, and grasslands that facilitate wildlife movement and compensate for habitat fragmentation. Managed wetlands are of sufficient size to maintain abundant wildlife populations. Grasslands consist of a sustainable mix of native and desirable nonnative species that support a variety of grassland-dependent species. The Refuge reduces further habitat fragmentation and buffers the effects of urbanization on agricultural lands and adjacent natural areas within the Delta region.

The Refuge pursues a land conservation program that complements other regional efforts and initiatives. Management efforts expand and diversify habitats for migratory birds and a range of species at risk. The Refuge promotes cooperative farming opportunities and strives to maintain traditional agricultural practices in southwestern Sacramento County that have proven benefits for migratory birds experiencing declines, such as long-billed curlews (*Numenius americanus*), Swainson's hawks (*Buteo swainsoni*) and sandhill cranes (*Grus canadensis*). Through cooperation with other agencies, conservation organizations, neighbors, and other partners, the Refuge develops and manages wetlands in a manner that reflects historic hydrologic patterns and is consistent with local, State, and Federal floodplain management goals and programs.

Stone Lakes was established as a national wildlife refuge because of passionate support from people who recognized its ecological importance and critical role for the floodplain of the Beach-Stone Lakes basin.. The community sees the Refuge as a sanctuary for fish, wildlife and the habitats upon which they depend, a site for recreation and learning and a natural setting that can enrich their lives according to their values. Visitors representing the area's diversity enjoy increasing opportunities for accessible recreation that harmonizes with Refuge conservation efforts, such as hunting, fishing, wildlife observation and photography. The education community looks to the Refuge as a key partner in environmental education programming. Volunteers from all walks of life find an outlet for their interests and talents in a responsive and appreciative setting.

Disclaimer

CCPs provide long term guidance for management decisions and set forth goals, objectives, and strategies needed to accomplish refuge purposes and identify the Service's best estimate of future needs. These plans detail program planning levels that are sometimes substantially above current budget allocations and, as such, are primarily for Service strategic planning and program prioritization purposes. The plans do not constitute a commitment for staffing increases, operational and maintenance increases, or funding for future land acquisition.

Stone Lakes
National Wildlife Refuge

Draft Comprehensive Conservation Plan

Prepared by:

U.S. Fish and Wildlife Service
California/Nevada Refuge Planning Office
2800 Cottage Way, W-1832
Sacramento, CA 95825

Stone Lakes National Wildlife Refuge
1624 Hood-Franklin Road
Elk Grove, CA 95758

September 2006

Approved by: _____ **Date**_____
California/Nevada Operations Manager

Contents

Figures

Tables

Appendices 107

Acronyms

California Department of Boating and Waterways	DBW
California Department of Fish and Game	DFG
California Department of Water Resources	DWR
California Endangered Species Act	CESA
Comprehensive Conservation Plan	CCP
California Department of Transportation	Caltrans
California Department of Parks and Recreation	DPR
California Native Plant Society	CNPS
Endangered Species Act	ESA
Environmental Assessment	EA
Environmental Impact Statement	EIS
Global positioning system	GPS
Memorandum of Agreement	MOA
Memorandum of Understanding	MOU
National Wildlife Refuge	Refuge
National Wildlife Refuge System	Refuge System
National Wildlife Refuge System Improvement Act of 1977	Improvement Act
Natural Resources Conservation Service	NRCS
National Environmental Policy Act	NEPA
Native American Grave Protection and Repatriation Act	NAGPRA
Sacramento-San Joaquin Delta	Delta
Stone Lakes National Wildlife Refuge	Refuge
Sacramento Regional County Sanitation District	SRCSD
State Water Resources Control Board	SWRCB
Sacramento Regional Wastewater Treatment Plant	SRWTP
Sacramento-Yolo Mosquito and Vector Control District	SYMVCD
University of California	UC
U.S. Army Corps of Engineers	USACE
U.S. Environmental Protection Agency	USEPA
U.S. Fish and Wildlife Service	Service
U.S. Department of Agriculture	USDA
U. S. Geological Survey	USGS

1 Introduction

Introduction

Stone Lakes National Wildlife Refuge (Refuge) was established in 1994, becoming the 505th refuge in the National Wildlife Refuge System (NWRS). The Refuge boundary encompasses about 17,640 acres; this includes a core Refuge area of about 9,000 acres and a 9,000 acre "Cooperative Wildlife Management Area" where the Service first seeks to enter into cooperative agreements and memoranda of understanding with landowners or purchase conservation easements.. The Service actively manages about 6,200 acres. The Refuge is located in the Beach-Stone Lakes Basin within the Sacramento Valley in southwestern Sacramento County; it lies about ten miles south of the city of Sacramento, straddling Interstate-5 from the town of Freeport south to Lost Slough.

Purpose and Need for the Comprehensive Conservation Plan (CCP)

The Service prepared this draft CCP to guide management of fish, wildlife, plants, other natural resources and visitor use on the Refuge for the next 15 years. The Comprehensive Conservation Plan (CCP) is flexible; it will be revised periodically to ensure that its goals, objectives, implementation strategies and timetables remain valid and appropriate. Major revisions require and provide a process for public involvement and National Environmental Policy Act (NEPA) review, if needed.

The NWRS Improvement Act of 1997 requires that the Service develop a CCP for each refuge by 2012, and that refuges be managed in a way that ensures the long-term conservation of fish, wildlife, plants, and their habitats and provides for compatible wildlife-dependent recreation. The purposes for developing a CCP are:
- Provide a clear statement of direction for the future management
- Provide long-term continuity in Refuge Complex management;
- Communicate the U.S. Fish and Wildlife Service's management priorities for the Refuges to their conservation partners, neighbors, visitors, and the general public;
- Provide an opportunity for the public to help shape the future management of the Refuges;
- Ensure that management programs on the Refuges are consistent with the mandates of the National Wildlife Refuge System (Refuge System) and the purposes for which each Refuge was established;
- Ensure that the management of the Refuges fully considers resource priorities and management strategies identified in other Federal, State, and local plans;
- Provide a basis for budget requests to support the Refuge's needs staffing, operations, maintenance, and capital improvements; and
- Evaluate existing and proposed uses of each refuge to ensure that they are compatible with the refuge purpose(s) as well as the maintenance of biological integrity, diversity, and environmental health.

U.S. Fish and Wildlife Service and National Wildlife Refuge System
U.S. Fish and Wildlife Service Responsibilities

The U.S. Fish and Wildlife Service (Service) is the primary Federal agency responsible for conserving and enhancing the nation's fish and wildlife populations and their habitats. Although this responsibility is shared with other Federal, State, Tribal, local, and private entities, the Service has specific responsibilities for migratory birds, threatened and endangered species, inter-jurisdictional fish and certain marine mammals. The Service has similar responsibilities for the lands and waters it administers to support the conservation and enhancement of fish and wildlife.

The National Wildlife Refuge System

The National Wildlife Refuge System (NWRS) is the largest system of lands in the world dedicated to the conservation of

The Service has specific responsibilities for migratory birds such as this great egret.
Photo by Tom Harvey, USFWS

fish and wildlife. Operated and managed by the Service, it currently includes 545 refuges with a combined area of more than 94 million acres. The majority of refuge lands (over 77 million acres) are located in Alaska. The remaining acreage is scattered across the other 49 states and several island territories. About 20.6 million acres are managed as wilderness under the Wilderness Act of 1964.

The NWRS started in 1903, when President Theodore Roosevelt protected an island with nesting pelicans, herons, ibis, and roseate spoonbills in Florida's Indian River from feather collectors decimating their colonies. He established Pelican Island as the nation's first bird sanctuary and went on to establish many other sanctuaries for wildlife during his tenure. This small network of sanctuaries continued to expand, later becoming the NWRS. In contrast to other public lands, which are managed for multiple uses, refuges are specifically managed for fish and wildlife conservation.

The mission of the NWRS, established by the NWRS Improvement Act of 1997, is:

"To administer a national network of lands and waters for the conservation, management, and where appropriate, restoration of the fish, wildlife, and plant resources and their habitats within the United States for the benefit of present and future generations of Americans."

The goals of the NWRS, as established by the Draft Policy on the NWRS (January 16, 2001), are:

- To fulfill our statutory duty to achieve refuge purpose(s) and further the System mission.
- Conserve, restore where appropriate, and enhance all species of fish, wildlife, and plants that are endangered or threatened with becoming endangered.
- Perpetuate migratory bird, interjurisdictional fish, and marine mammal populations.
- Conserve a diversity of fish, wildlife, and plants.
- Conserve and restore where appropriate representative ecosystems of the United States, including ecological processes characteristic of those ecosystems.
- Foster understanding and instill appreciation of native fish, wildlife, and plants and their conservation by providing the public with safe, high-quality, and compatible wildlife-dependent visitor use. Such use includes hunting, fishing, wildlife observation and photography, and environmental education and interpretation.

Legal and Policy Guidance

Legal mandates and Service policies govern the Service's planning and management of the NWRS. A list and brief description can be found at the "Division of Congressional and Legislative Affairs, USFWS" Web site (http://laws.fws.gov). In addition, the Service has developed draft or final policies to guide NWRS planning and management. These policies can be found at the "NWRS Policies" Web site (http://www.fws.gov/refuges/policymakers/nwrpolicies.html). The main sources of legal and policy guidance for the CCP and EA are described below.

National Wildlife Refuge System Improvement Act of 1997

Statutory authority for Service management and associated habitat management planning on units of the NWRS is derived from the National Wildlife Refuge System Administration Act of 1966 (Refuge Administration Act), which was significantly amended by the National Wildlife Refuge System Improvement Act of 1997 (Refuge Improvement Act, 16 U.S.C. 668dd-668ee). Section 4(a)(3) of the Refuge Improvement Act states, "With respect to the National Wildlife System [NWRS], it is the policy of the United States that – (A) each refuge shall be managed to fulfill the mission of the System, as well as the specific purposes for which that refuge was established…" The Refuge Improvement Act also states that the "…purposes of the refuge and purposes for each refuge mean the purposes specified in or derived from law, proclamation, executive order, agreement, public land order, donation document, or administrative memorandum establishing, authorizing, or expanding a refuge, refuge unit, or refuge subunit."

The Refuge Administration Act, as amended, clearly establishes wildlife conservation as the core NWRS mission. House Report 105-106, accompanying the Refuge Improvement Act, states "…the fundamental mission of our System is wildlife conservation: "… wildlife and wildlife conservation must come first." In contrast to some other systems of federal lands which are managed on a sustained-yield basis for multiple uses, the NWRS is a primary-use network of lands and waters. First and foremost, refuges are managed for fish, wildlife, plants, and their habitats. In addition, units of the NWRS are legally closed to all public access and use, including economic uses, unless and until they are officially opened through an analytical, public process called the refuge compatibility process. With the exception of refuge management activities which are not economic in nature, all other uses are subservient to the NWRS' primary wildlife management responsibility and they must be determined compatible before being authorized.

The Refuge Improvement Act provides clear standards for management, use, planning, and growth of the NWRS. Its passage followed the promulgation of Executive Order 12996 (April 1996), "Management of Public Uses on National Wildlife Refuges", reflecting the importance of conserving natural resources for the benefit of present and future generations of people. The Refuge Improvement Act recognizes that wildlife-dependent recreational uses including hunting, fishing, wildlife observation and photography, and environmental education and interpretation, when determined to be compatible with the mission of the System and purposes of the Refuge, are legitimate and appropriate public uses of the Refuge System. Section 5 (C) and (D) of the Refuge Improvement Act states "compatible wildlife-dependent recreational uses are the priority general public uses of the Refuge System and shall receive priority consideration in planning and management; and when the Secretary determines that a proposed wildlife-dependent recreational use is a compatible use within a refuge, that activity should be facilitated, subject to such restrictions or regulations as may be necessary, reasonable, and appropriate."

The Refuge Improvement Act also directs the Service to maintain adequate water quantity and quality to fulfill the NWRS mission and refuge purposes, and to acquire, under state law, water rights that are needed for refuge purposes.

Compatibility Policy

Lands within the NWRS are different from other multiple use public lands in that they are closed to all visitor uses unless specifically and legally opened. The Improvement Act states ". . . the Secretary shall not initiate or permit a new use of a Refuge or expand, renew, or extend an existing use of a Refuge, unless the Secretary has determined that the use is a compatible use and that the use is not inconsistent with public safety." The Improvement Act also states that ". . . compatible wildlife-dependent recreational uses (hunting, fishing, wildlife observation and photography, or environmental education and interpretation) are the priority general public uses of the System and shall receive priority consideration in Refuge planning and management."

In accordance with the Improvement Act, the Service has adopted a Compatibility Policy (603 FW 2) that includes guidelines for determining if a use proposed on a national wildlife refuge is compatible with the purposes for which the refuge was established. A compatible use is defined in the policy as a proposed or existing wildlife-dependent recreational use or any other use of a national wildlife refuge that, based on sound professional judgment, will not materially interfere with or detract from the fulfillment of the NWRS mission or the purposes for which the Refuge was established and contributes to the maintenance of biological integrity, diversity, and environmental health. The Policy also includes procedures for documentation and periodic review of existing refuge uses.

When a determination is made as to whether a proposed use is compatible or not, this determination is provided in writing and is referred to as a compatibility determination. An opportunity for public review and comment is required for all compatibility determinations. For compatibility determinations prepared concurrently with a CCP or step-down management plan, the opportunity for public review and comment is provided during the public review period for the draft plan and associated NEPA document. The Refuge has completed draft compatibility determinations for fishing, wildlife observation and photography, environmental education and interpretation, high speed boating, recreational boating, research, grazing, plant collecting, and mosquito monitoring and control. These compatibility determinations will be finalized with the CCP. The compatibility determinations prepared in association with this draft CCP/EA are provided in Appendix A.

Biological Integrity, Diversity, and Environmental Health Policy

Section 4(a)(4)(B) of the Refuge Improvement Act states, "In administering the System, the Secretary shall…ensure that the biological integrity, diversity, and environmental health of the System are maintained for the benefit of present and future generations of Americans…" This legislative mandate represents an additional directive to be followed while achieving refuge purposes and the NWRS mission. The Act requires the consideration and protection of a broad spectrum of fish, wildlife, plant, and habitat resources found on a refuge. Service policy guiding implementation of this statutory requirement provides a refuge manager with an evaluation process to analyze his/her refuge and recommend the best management direction to prevent further degradation of environmental conditions; and, where appropriate, and in concert with refuge purposes and NWRS mission, to restore lost or severely degraded resource components. Within the Biological Integrity, Diversity, and Environmental Health Policy (601 FW 3[3.7B]), the relationships among biological integrity, diversity, and environmental health; NWRS mission; and refuge purposes are explained as follows, "…each refuge will be managed to fulfill refuge purpose(s) as well as to help fulfill the System mission, and we will accomplish these purpose(s) and our mission by ensuring that the biological integrity, diversity, and environmental health of each refuge are maintained and where appropriate, restored."

When evaluating the appropriate management direction for refuges, Refuge Managers will use sound professional judgment to determine their refuge's contribution to biological integrity, diversity, and environmental health at multiple landscape scales. Sound professional judgment incorporates field experience, an understanding of the refuge's role within an ecosystem, and the knowledge of refuge resources, applicable laws and best available science, including consultation with resource experts both inside and outside of the Service.

The priority visitor uses of the NWRS are not in conflict with this policy when they have been determined to be compatible. The directives of this policy do not envision or necessitate the exclusion of visitors or the elimination of visitor use structures from refuges; however, maintenance and/or restoration of biological integrity, diversity, and environmental health may require spatial or temporal zoning of visitor use programs and associated infrastructures. General success in maintaining or restoring biological integrity, diversity, and environmental health will produce higher quality opportunities for providing wildlife-dependent recreational uses.

Draft Wilderness Stewardship Policy Pursuant to the Wilderness Act of 1964

This policy updates guidance on administrative and public activities on wilderness and proposed wilderness within the NWRS. The purpose of the policy is to prescribe how the Service:
"preserves the character and qualities of designated wilderness while managing for the refuge establishing purpose(s), maintains outstanding opportunities for solitude and primitive and unconfined type of recreation, and conducts minimum requirements analyses before taking any action that may impact wilderness character."

The policy emphasizes recreational uses that are compatible and wilderness-dependent. The policy clarifies conditions upon which generally prohibited uses (motor vehicles, motorized equipment, mechanical transport, structures, and installations) may be necessary for wilderness protection. It confirms that:
"we will generally not modify habitat, species population levels, or natural ecological processes in refuge wilderness unless doing so maintains or restores ecological integrity that has been degraded by human influence or is necessary to protect or recover threatened or endangered species."

National Environmental Policy Act of 1969

This Draft CCP and associated National Environmental Policy Act (NEPA) document has been prepared consistent with the requirements of NEPA, the Council on Environmental Quality (CEQ) NEPA regulations (40 CFR Secs. 1500 et seq.), and the Department of Interior's NEPA procedures (Department Manual, Part 516).

Stone Lakes National Wildlife Refuge
Location
The Refuge is located in southern Sacramento County, west of the city of Elk Grove. It lies within the Morrison Creek, Cosumnes River and Mokelumne River watersheds as well as the Sacramento-San Joaquin Delta (Delta) (Figure 1. Ecoregion and Watershed Map). The approved Refuge boundary is roughly defined by Morrison Creek to the north, Franklin Boulevard and Interstate-5 to the east, the former Southern Pacific Railroad to the west and Lost Slough to the south.

Refuge Setting
Before European settlement, the Beach-Stone Lakes Basin was a magnet for wildlife, such as elk (*Cervus elaphus*), pronghorn (*Antilocapra americana*) and grizzly bear (*Ursus arctos horribilis*). During winter storms, the flooded basin could stretch from lower Morrison Creek to the Mokelumne River, expanding lakes and seasonal wetlands that supported tens of thousands of migratory birds. The land destined to become a national wildlife refuge teemed with wildlife.

The Plains Miwok relied on the land, its plants and its abundant wildlife for survival. These American Indians camped, hunted and fished along the shores of the area's lakes. Historic Beach Lake once covered nearly 1,000 acres and North and South Stone Lakes were also extensive. Located in the heart of the Refuge, the lakes received their names in the mid 1800s from a former landowner, a Sacramento merchant named Rockwell Stone. The Stone family held about 1,000 acres until 1891.

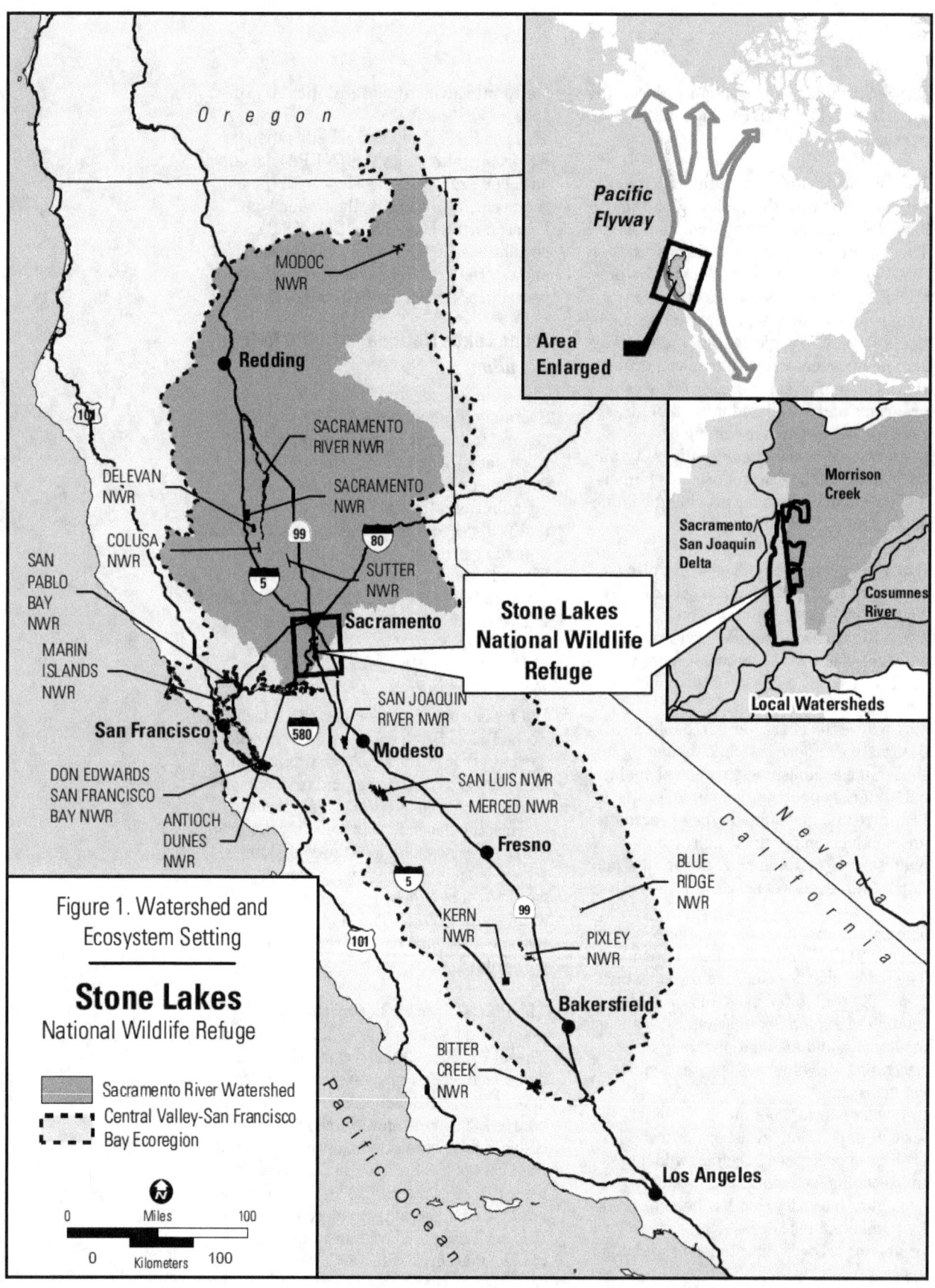

Figure 1. Watershed and Ecosystem Setting

Stone Lakes
National Wildlife Refuge

Sacramento River Watershed

Central Valley-San Francisco Bay Ecoregion

Miles
0   100

Kilometers
0   100

Changes began in the mid 1800s. Levees were constructed along the Sacramento River and around Delta islands so the land could be farmed. The Southern Pacific Railroad was built, bisecting the basin, allowing nearly complete drainage of its lakes. Finally, Interstate-5 was constructed, ushering in tremendous pressure for urban development.

As Sacramento grew in the mid 1960s, the U.S. Army Corps of Engineers (USACE) suggested building channels in the area to hold floodwaters. Conservation organizations also became interested in the basin in late 1960s, hoping to avoid a major flood control project and keep the area natural. During the same period, a local landowner proposed build a new town for 50,000 people around North Stone Lake.

In response to these pressures and in recognition of the importance of the Stone Lakes Basin floodplain, the State of California and County of Sacramento purchased about 2,600 acres in the 1970s, turning the land over to their respective park departments to manage.

By the late 1980s the idea of further protecting the Stone Lakes Basin by establishing a national wildlife refuge took hold. Support for the Refuge derived partly from the fact that the unique lakes and waterways of the basin lie entirely within the 100-year floodplain. The basin also occupies a strategic location for buffering the effects of urban encroachment into the Delta. Additionally, a national wildlife refuge could potentially provide a link with ongoing nearby land conservation efforts such as the Cosumnes River Preserve.

Several local legislators supported protecting the land from development and were in a position to help move the process forward.

History of Refuge Establishment and Acquisition
In July 1992, the Service completed a complex two year public planning process resulting in finalization of an Environmental Impact Statement (EIS). The EIS (USFWS 1992) defined the present 18,000 acre approved Refuge boundary.

During circulation of the draft EIS, , the Service received written and verbal input from over 6,000 citizens about potential effects a refuge could have on the landscape and the EIS' adequacy in addressing these issues. Despite litigation under NEPA over the adequacy of the EIS , the Service successfully defended its Record of Decision and with a broad base of local support, established the Refuge in 1992.

With acquisition of the first property in 1994, the Refuge was officially established as the 505th unit in the National Wildlife Refuge System. It joined the ranks of other local land conservation and management projects, including the Cosumnes River Preserve to the southeast and the Vic Fazio Yolo Bypass Wildlife Area to the west, which have similar goals of protecting and enhancing vital Central Valley fish and wildlife habitats.

With a broad base of local support the Refuge was established in 1992, protecting habitat for native species like this red-shouldered hawk.
Photo by Tom Harvey, USFWS

Land Protection
The approved boundary for the Refuge--the area within which the Service is authorized to work with willing landowners to acquire and/or manage land is 17,640.7 acres (Figure 2. Land Status). The Refuge consists of a 9,146 acre core area (Figure 3. Core and Cooperative Wildlife Management Areas), encompassing Upper and Lower Beach Lakes and North and South Stone Lakes and a 9,066 acre Cooperative Wildlife Management Area (CWMA), encompassing lands to the east and south of the core area. Within the approved Refuge Boundary, the Service may pursue a number of approaches

to conserve and manage lands, depending on the preferences of willing landowners. These may include: technical assistance, cooperative agreements, memoranda of understanding and acquisition of conservation or agricultural easements and fee title interest. In the EIS (USFWS 1992), the Service agreed to use fee title acquisition within the CWMA only on a case by case basis and after seeking approval by the Sacramento County Board of Supervisors. The preferred approaches to conserve lands within the CWMA are: cooperative agreements, memoranda of understanding, and purchase of conservation or agricultural easements. According to the August 1992 Land Protection Plan for The Refuge, a primary objective of the CWMA is to maintain lands in private ownership and continue agricultural production (Land Protection Plan, Appendix B).

To date, the Service manages about 6,200 acres within the approved project boundary including: 2,933 acres under cooperative agreement; 1,740 acres in fee title ownership; and 1,533 acres under agricultural easement.

The Service is also exploring cooperative management of an additional 2,210 acres within the approved boundary that are owned by two other agencies: (1) Sacramento Regional Sanitation District (1,800 acres); and (2) California Department of Water Resources (410 acres).

Land Conservation Methods

Working with willing landowners and local and state agencies, the Service may use various means to conserve or manage fish and wildlife and their habitats within the approved Refuge boundary. These may include: fee title acquisition, conservation easements, memoranda of understanding and cooperative agreements, financial incentives and technical assistance and education and outreach. It is the established policy of the Service to seek the minimum degree of interest in property needed to accomplish refuge land conservation objectives.

In fee title acquisitions, the Service acquires full ownership of property through fee simple purchase, donation, exchange, or transfer from another Federal agency. Land acquired in fee title by the Service is removed from county tax roles. To partially offset this loss, the Service provides annual payments to counties as authorized by the Refuge Revenue Sharing Act (Public Law 95-469). The Service is required under the U.S. Constitution to pay fair market value for property and purchases are dependent on the availability of funds.

In acquiring a conservation easement, the Service purchases the minimum rights needed to conserve fish and wildlife habitat, while allowing the existing landowner to retain title to the land. Easements may include wetland or waterfowl habitat easements, upland easements, agricultural practices easements and non-development easements. The easement interest acquired by the Service becomes part of the Refuge and is subject to applicable laws and regulations pertaining to refuges. The easement is a permanent interest in the property that runs with the land and the landowner remains responsible for all property taxes About 5,000 acres within the approved Refuge boundary and CWMA are currently publicly owned and managed for conservation purposes by five local and State agencies. A majority of these lands are or will be jointly managed with the Service through memoranda of understanding and cooperative agreements.

The Service may also assist in securing financial incentives for landowners who are not willing to sell an interest in their property but wish to explore conservation or enhancement of fish and wildlife habitats on their property. For example, through the Partners for Fish and Wildlife program, landowners may apply for financial assistance from the Service to protect, enhance, or restore wetland, riparian, or native grassland habitats on their property. In addition, the Service could assist a landowner to secure funds from Farm Bill programs available from the U.S. Department of Agriculture/Natural

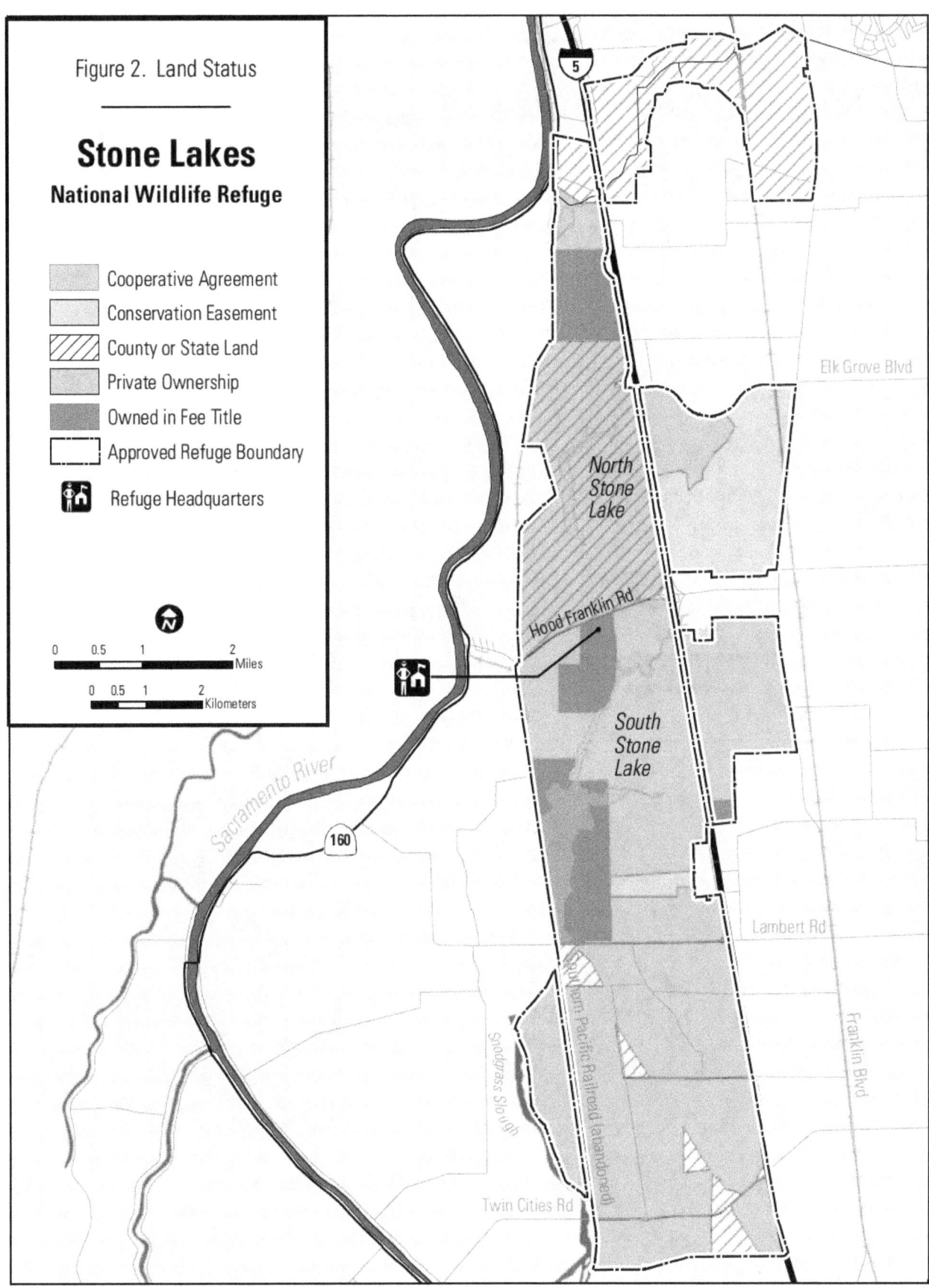

Figure 2. Land Status

Stone Lakes
National Wildlife Refuge

Cooperative Agreement
Conservation Easement
County or State Land
Private Ownership
Owned in Fee Title
Approved Refuge Boundary
Refuge Headquarters

0   0.5   1   2
Miles

0   0.5   1   2
Kilometers

North
Stone
Lake

South
Stone
Lake

Hood Franklin Rd

Elk Grove Blvd

Lambert Rd

Franklin Blvd

Sacramento River

160

Snodgrass Slough

Southern Pacific Railroad (abandoned)

Twin Cities Rd

5

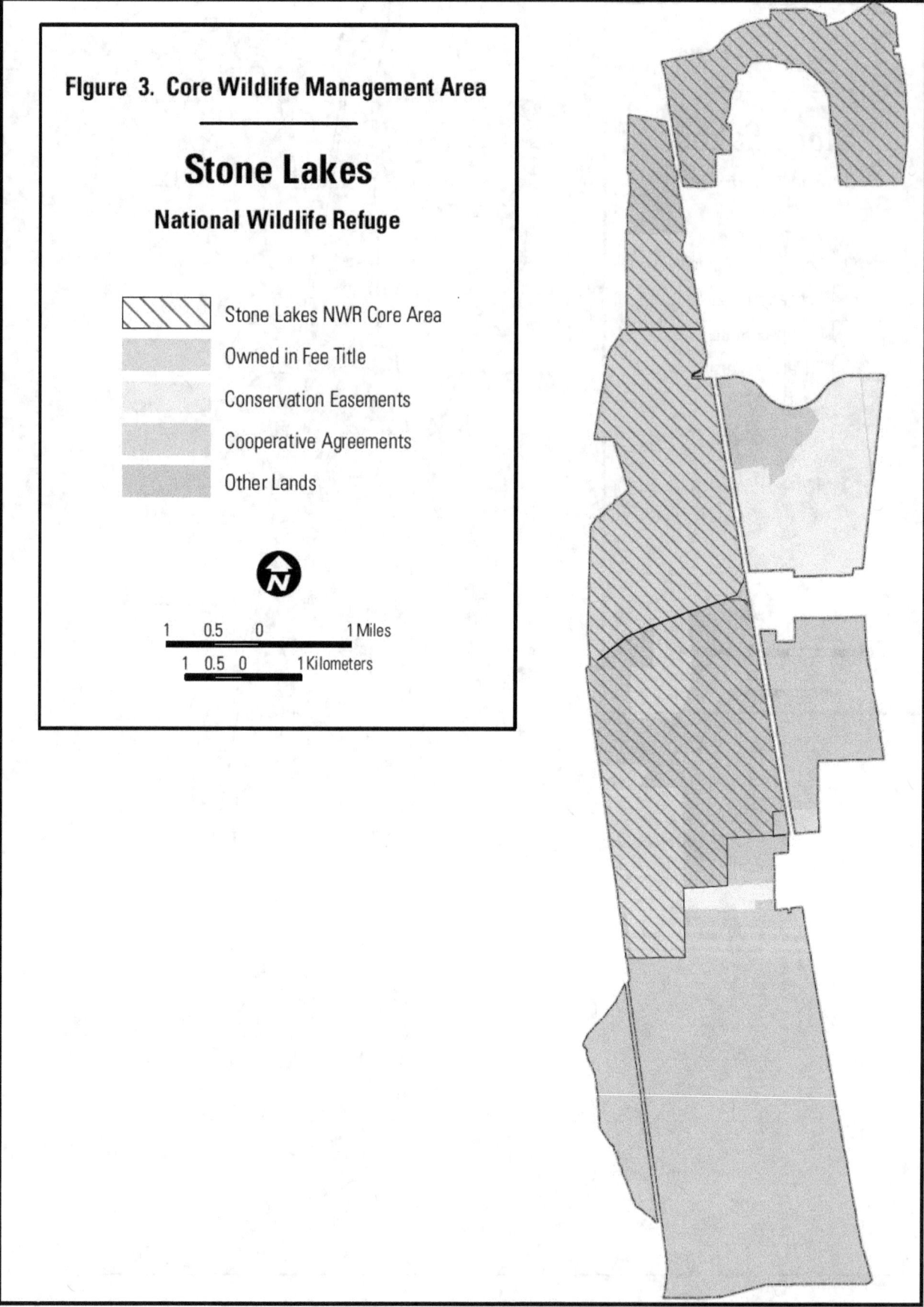

Figure 3. Core Wildlife Management Area

Stone Lakes
National Wildlife Refuge

Stone Lakes NWR Core Area

Owned in Fee Title

Conservation Easements

Cooperative Agreements

Other Lands

N

1   0.5   0   1 Miles

1   0.5   0   1 Kilometers

Resources Conservation Service (NRCS). Potential NRCS programs that could benefit landowners and further Refuge land conservation objectives include the: Conservation of Private Grazing Land Program, Environmental Quality Incentives Program, Farmland Protection Program, Wetlands Reserve Program and Wildlife Habitat Incentives Program. Finally, Service staff is available to provide technical assistance and education and outreach information to willing landowners who are interested in conserving fish and wildlife habitats on their lands.

The Refuge has financed most of its land acquisition and restoration efforts with grants from a wide range of state and federal agencies and private organizations. These sources have played a vital role in advancing the Refuge's land conservation and management programs. Grants have been provided by: City of Sacramento, County of Sacramento, California Wildlife Conservation Board, California Environmental Enhancement Mitigation Fund, California Environmental License Plate Fund, Cigarette and Tobacco Product Surtax, Department of Transportation-TEA 21 Fund, CALFED Bay Delta Program, North American Wetlands Conservation Act, Land and Water Conservation Fund, Central Valley Project Improvement Act, National Fish and Wildlife Foundation, David and Lucille Packard Foundation, The Trust for Public Land and other private donations.

Partnerships

Partnerships have been a cornerstone of Refuge development and management. A consortium of public and private organizations strongly supported the designation of Stone Lakes as a national wildlife refuge and has since been joined by many others as the Refuge has expanded. The Refuge's urban location and the local and state agencies that own land within the Refuge boundary have provided numerous opportunities for partnerships from the Refuge's inception.

The Refuge staff routinely discusses and coordinates restoration activities, jointly applies for grants and discusses other management issues with the Sacramento County Department of Regional Parks, Recreation and Open Space (North Stone Lake Unit), the Sacramento Regional County Sanitation District (Bufferlands) and the California Departments of Transportation (Caltrans) (Beach Lake Mitigation Bank), California Department of Parks and Recreation (DPR) (North Stone Lake Unit) and California Department of Water Resources (DWR) . The Service has finalized a cooperative agreement with Sacramento County Department of Regional Parks, Recreation and Open Space over management of the North Stone Lake unit and partners closely with Sacramento Regional County Sanitation District on the annual event, Walk on the Wildside, and the water hyacinth control program. .

Controlling water hyacinth a nonnative, invasive aquatic plant, has been a prime motivation for formation of an important partnership, the Stone Lakes Water Hyacinth Working Group, in which the Refuge plays a central role. This group includes more than a dozen local and state agencies, organizations, and private individuals who own or manage land in the Stone Lakes Basin, affected by this noxious weed. Recent partners in the group have included: the Refuge, California Department of Boating and Waterways (DBW), Sacramento Regional County Sanitation District (SRCSD), Sacramento County Supervisor Don Notolli, Sacramento County Department of Water Resources, Sacramento County Agricultural Commission, Sacramento-Yolo Mosquito and Vector Control District (SYMVCD), Florin Resource Conservation District, Caltrans, Vino Farms, the Whitney Family, LaRue Schock and the San Francisco Estuary Institute. The working group cooperates on eradication, has applied for and received grants and has produced educational materials to reduce the spread of water hyacinth in local waterways.

Controlling and eliminating invasive water hyacinth, shown here being removed from Lambert Ditch by volunteers, was the prime motivation for another important partnership: the Stone Lakes Water Hyacinth Working Group.
Photo by USFWS

The Refuge also coordinates with California Departments of Fish and Game (DFG) and DBW , Resource Conservation District #813 and Sacramento County Department of Environmental Review on issues of mutual management concern. Much of the restoration that has occurred on Refuge managed land occurred through partnerships with a variety of private organization, including Ducks Unlimited, California Waterfowl Association, Wildlands, Inc., Stone Lakes National Wildlife Refuge Association, American Lands Conservancy, Sacramento Tree Foundation, Safari Club, and Trust for Public Land.

The Service entered into a Memorandum of Understanding (MOU) with SYMVCD in 1993 to address concerns regarding potential effects the Refuge may have on mosquito populations. According to the MOU, the Service agreed to consult with SYMVCD on the design and management of Refuge wetlands and provide access to SYMVCD to monitor the mosquito population on the Refuge. The Service also agreed to submit Pesticide Use Proposals for pesticides SYMVCD may wish to use on the Refuge, if thresholds for larval or adult control are exceeded. SYMVCD and the Service rely on a full range of integrated pest management techniques to manage mosquito populations, including water and vegetation management, biological control (e.g., planting of mosquito fish [*Gambusia affinis*]) and if necessary,

chemical control of larval or adult mosquitos. As a result, mosquito larval control activities since 1994 have been largely limited to localized (less than five acres) applications of larvicides and until 2005, and only three applications of an adulticides.

In 2005, West Nile Virus (WNV) became established in Sacramento and Yolo counties, triggering aggressive and widespread mosquito control efforts. In August of 2005 the number of human WNV cases and rate of infected adult mosquitos were so high that SYMVCD conducted aerial applications of pyrethrin over a major portion of Sacramento County (Sacramento County 2006). During 2005, the Refuge received ultra-low volume (ULV) ground treatments of pyrethrin on 18 occasions from September 28 through October 12. As of July 2006, the Refuge has been adulticided six times between June 27 and July 21.

The Service also cooperates with SYMVCD in the monitoring of landbird populations on the Refuge, primarily to evaluate the role of wild bird populations as reservoirs of mosquito-borne diseases, such as western equine encephalitis, St. Louis encephalitis, and West Nile Virus. The landbird monitoring program began in 1995 and involves mist netting and banding of a wide variety of birds. A small blood sample (0.10 cc) is taken from some species for disease analysis. In addition to contributing to the goals of mosquito management, the program has provided valuable information regarding bird use on the Refuge, timing of migration, reproductive ecology and reproductive success.

In addition to those already mentioned, several programs and nongovernmental organizations (NGOs) provide vital support for Refuge land conservation, restoration and visitor services programs, including the CALFED Bay Delta Authority Ecological Restoration Program, Central Valley Project Improvement Act, North American Wetlands Conservation Act, Audubon California, California Native Plant Society, California Waterfowl Association, The Nature Conservancy and Sacramento

Open Space. These groups routinely assist with grant writing and fundraising, coordinate research or census efforts, help with planning programs and activities and provide coverage of Refuge activities in their publications or events.

Refuge Purposes

Lands within the Refuge System are acquired and managed under a variety of legislative acts and administrative orders and authorities. The official purpose or purposes for a refuge are specified in or derived from the law, proclamation, executive order, agreement, public land order, funding source, donation document, or administrative memorandum establishing, authorizing, or expanding a refuge, refuge unit, or refuge subunit. The purpose of a refuge is defined when it is established or when new land is added to an existing refuge. When an addition to a refuge is acquired under an authority different from the authority used to establish the original refuge, the addition takes on the purposes of the original refuge, but the original refuge does not take on the purposes of the addition. Refuge managers must consider all of the purposes. However, purposes that deal with the conservation, management, and restoration of fish, wildlife and plants and their habitats take precedent over other purposes in the management and administration of a refuge.

The Refuge System Improvement Act directs the Service to manage each refuge to fulfill the mission of the Refuge System, as well as the specific purposes for which that refuge was established. Refuge purposes are the driving force in developing refuge vision statements, goals, objectives and strategies in the CCP. Refuge purposes are also critical to determining the compatibility of all existing and proposed refuge uses.

Stone Lakes National Wildlife Refuge was established under the authority of the Emergency Wetlands Resources Act of 1986, the Fish and Wildlife Act of 1956, The Migratory Bird Conservation Act and The Endangered Species Act of 1973.

According to these authorities, the primary Refuge-wide purposes are:

"... for the conservation of the wetlands of the Nation in order to maintain the public benefits they provide and to help fulfill international obligations contained in various migratory bird treaties and conventions ..." 16 U.S.C. §§ 3901(b) (Emergency Wetlands Resources Act of 1986)

"... for the development, advancement, management, conservation, and protection of fish and wildlife resources ..." 16 U.S.C. §§ 742f(a)(4) (Fish and Wildlife Act of 1956)

"... for the benefit of the United States Fish and Wildlife Service, in performing its activities and services. Such acceptance may be subject to the terms of any restrictive or affirmative covenant, or condition of servitude ..." 16 U.S.C. §§ 742f(b)(1) (Fish and Wildlife Act of 1956)

"... for use as an inviolate sanctuary, or for any other management purpose, for migratory birds." 16 U.S.C. §§ 715d (Migratory Bird Conservation Act)

"... to conserve (A) fish or wildlife which are listed as endangered species or threatened species .... or (B) plants ..." 16 U.S.C. §§ 1534 (Endangered Species Act of 1973)

Related Projects and Studies in the Area

U.S. Fish and Wildlife Service

Final Environmental Impact Statement Stone Lakes National Wildlife Refuge (EIS). In 1972, Jones and Stokes Associates prepared an EIS for the Refuge. The purpose of the EIS was to evaluate the effects of various Service alternatives to acquire and protect lands in southwestern Sacramento County to establish the Refuge. The EIS includes interim Refuge management goals and proposed habitat restoration areas.

The interim Refuge management goals are as follows:

- Preserve, enhance, and restore a diverse assemblage of native Central Valley plant communities and their associated fish, wildlife and plants;
- Preserve, enhance, and restore habitat to maintain and assist in the recovery of rare, threatened, and endangered plants and animals;
- Preserve, enhance, and restore wetlands and adjacent agricultural lands to provide foraging and sanctuary habitat needed to achieve the distribution and population levels of migratory waterfowl and other water birds consistent with the goals and objectives of the North American Waterfowl Management Plan and Central Valley Habitat Joint Venture;
- Create linkages between refuge habitats and habitats on adjacent lands to reverse past impacts of habitat fragmentation on wildlife and plants;
- Coordinate refuge land acquisition and management activities with other agencies and organizations to maximize the effectiveness of refuge contributions to regional habitat needs;
- Provide for environmental education, interpretation and fish and wildlife oriented recreation in an urban setting accessible to large populations; and
- Manage riverine wetlands and adjacent floodplain lands in a manner consistent with local, State and Federal flood management; sediment and erosion control, and water quality objectives.

Draft North Stone Lake Management and Restoration Plan. The 2,791 acre North Stone Lake Unit consists of two adjacent parcels owned by the DPR (1,224 acres) and Sacramento County (1,567 acres). The goal of the Service is to cooperatively manage both these properties with the County and the State, as a unit of the Refuge. The Service currently has a cooperative agreement with Sacramento County for management of their property and is drafting an agreement with DPR that addresses the State-owned land. Since Sacramento County has managed both parcels collectively as the North Stone Lake

Wildlife Refuge, they drafted a management and restoration plan in 1992. The plan has now been revised and updated by the Service. Some wetland restoration elements in the 1992 plan that were not considered to have neutral effects on floodplain storage were removed or modified in the revision but the plan has not been adopted by Sacramento County. . Under the revised draft plan, the North Stone Lake Unit would be managed for a diversity of native animal and plant species by enhancing and restoring a diversity of wetland and grassland habitats. Once completed, many of the restoration projects will require little management. Other restored habitats, such as seasonal marshes and grasslands, will require intensive management and manipulation.

Other Agencies and Projects

Sacramento Regional Wastewater Treatment Plant and Bufferlands. The Sacramento Regional County Sanitation District (SRCSD) constructed the Sacramento Regional Wastewater Treatment Plant (SRWTP) to treat wastewater for the urbanized area of Sacramento. In addition to constructing the plant, SRCSD purchased 2,650 acres surrounding the treatment plant to serve as a buffer between the plant and surrounding planned and existing residential communities. This land is known as the Bufferlands. Approximately 1,800 acres of the Bufferlands lie within the approved Refuge boundary The Service and SRCSD have drafted a cooperative management agreement for the Bufferlands to be managed a unit of the Refuge. SRCSD restores native habitats such as wetlands, riparian forest, and native grasslands and actively manages the Bufferlands as wildlife habitat. They also provide opportunities for; environmental education, interpretation, wildlife observation and fishing; oversee a volunteer program and partner with the Service and others on the annual Refuge event, Walk on the Wildside.

Vic Fazio Yolo Basin Wildlife Area. The Vic Fazio Yolo Wildlife Area is managed by the California Department of Fish and Game and located along Interstate-80 where

16,000 acres in the Yolo Bypass floodway have been restored to wetlands or support agricultural lands managed for the benefit of fish and wildlife. . The Wildlife Area lies approximately 15 miles northwest of the Refuge and was created through the cooperative efforts of an array of private, State and Federal partners. It covers approximately six square miles and provides visitor opportunities such as bird watching, outdoor educational programs and waterfowl hunting.

Cosumnes River Preserve. The Cosumnes River Preserve is located adjacent to and southeast of the Refuge's approved boundary and just upstream from the confluence of the Cosumnes and Mokelumne rivers. The Preserve was established through the cooperative efforts of a private/public partnership that includes The Nature Conservancy, Ducks Unlimited, U.S. Bureau of Land Management, Sacramento County and California Department of Water Resources. The project strives to conserve and enhance nearly 20,000 acres of riparian forest, wetlands and grasslands along the Cosumnes River, which is the only remaining un-dammed tributary of the Sacramento River.

The Cosumnes River floodplain provides habitat for tens of thousands of migratory waterfowl, songbirds and birds of prey; a large portion of the Central Valley's population of greater sandhill cranes (*Grus canadensis tabida*); and rare reptiles and mammals, such as the endangered giant garter snake (*Thamnophis gigas*). Chinook salmon (*Oncorhynchus tshawytscha*) and Pacific lamprey (*Lampetra tridentate*) spawn and native Delta fish breed and rear their young in the shallow waters of the wetlands.

The Central Valley Joint Venture. The Central Valley Joint Venture (CVJV) is a partnership of private conservation organizations and State and Federal agencies whose goal is to protect, maintain and restore habitat to increase Central Valley waterfowl populations to levels comparable to the 1970s and consistent with other objectives of the North American

Waterfowl Management Plan. The Central Valley of California is the most important waterfowl wintering area in the Pacific Flyway, supporting 60 percent of the flyway's duck and goose population. It is especially important that 65 percent of all pintails (*Anas acuta*) in the United States use the Central Valley.

CALFED Bay-Delta Authority (CALFED). CALFED, a consortium of stakeholders and State and Federal agencies, is attempting to develop a plan to address water supply and flood control concerns, as well as restoration of fish and wildlife populations of the Sacramento-San Joaquin Delta (Delta). Under CALFED's ecological restoration program funding was made available to purchase the Sun River portion of the South Stone Lake Unit.

Central Valley Project Improvement Act (CVPIA).
The CVPIA was adopted to incorporate conservation and enhancement of fish and wildlife populations into operation of the Central Valley Project by the U.S. Bureau of Reclamation. It provides for the allocation of water supplies for the recovery of native fishes and for State and Federal wildlife management areas. Funding available through the program assisted the Refuge with acquisition of the Headquarters Unit.

The Cosumnes River floodplain provides habitat for tens of thousands of migratory waterfowl, songbirds, and birds of prey; a large portion of the Central Valley's population of greater sandhill cranes; and uncommon reptiles and mammals, such as these river otters.
Photo by USFWS

2 The Planning Process

The Planning Process

The Refuge Planning Chapter of the Fish and Wildlife Service Manual (Part 602 FW 2.1, November 1996) and evolving policy related to the Refuge System Improvement Act of 1997 help to guide the process followed for developing this Comprehensive Conservation Plan (CCP). Key steps include:

- Gathering information;
- Initiating public involvement;
- Analyzing resource relationships;
- Identifying issues and developing vision and goals;
- Developing alternatives and assessing environmental effects;
- Identifying a preferred alternative;
- Publishing the draft CCP and NEPA document;
- Documenting public comments on the draft CCP;
- Revising the draft CCP and preparing the final CCP;
- Securing approval of the California/ Nevada Operations; and
- Implementing the CCP.

The CCP may be amended at any time, as necessary, under an adaptive management strategy. Public involvement and NEPA review will be required if major revisions are needed.

The Stone Lakes CCP Process

In a Federal Register Notice, dated August 26, 2002, the Service announced that it was preparing a CCP for the Refuge. The first Refuge planning update, distributed in July 2002, provided the public with background about the Refuge and the National Wildlife Refuge System and explained how CCP development fits into the overall picture of refuge management.

The second planning update, released in September 2002, announced a series of the public meetings and explained how the public could become involved in the planning process. The purpose of the meetings was to solicit public involvement in the CCP process and help Service staff identify issues and gather information to help develop the CCP.

This draft CCP and Environmental Assessment (EA) (Appendix C) are being distributed to Refuge cooperators, nearby landowners, State and Federal government agencies, local jurisdictions, private organizations, community groups and private citizens. The public has 30 days from the draft's release to provide comments. A final planning update will be issued at the same time as the final CCP. The draft CCP and EA can also be viewed at the following internet sites: http://stonelakes.fws.gov/ publicreview.htm and http://library.fws.gov/ ccps.htm.

The CCP will assist Refuge staff with preparation of annual work plans and updating the Refuge Operational Needs System (RONS) database. The RONS database describes the unfunded budget needs for each refuge and is the basis upon which funding increases are allocated for operational needs. The plan may also be reviewed during routine inspections or programmatic evaluations. Results of the reviews may indicate a need to modify the plan. Periodic review of the objectives and strategies is an integral part of the plan, and management activities may be modified if the desired results are not achieved. Depending on the degree that changes may be required, the appropriate level of public involvement and NEPA documentation will be determined by the Refuge Manager. The CCP will be formally revised every 15 years.

Issues Identified by the Public

During the CCP public scoping process, issues, concerns, and opportunities were identified through public meetings, discussions with planning team members and other key contacts. The public had an opportunity to attend four scoping meetings, in Elk Grove, Davis, Walnut Grove and Sacramento, where their comments were recorded. More than 135 people attended these meetings. Over 250 people also provided written comments by mail and email and through personal conversations with the Refuge and planning staffs. During the planning process, the Service has received numerous comments and suggestions regarding the potential for public hunting on the Refuge. Due to opportunities related to recent conveyance of the Sun River property to the Refuge and commitments by the Service to maintain hunting opportunities in the South Stone

Public comments, on Comprehensive Conservation Planning for the Refuge, were received in writing, via e-mail, via postal mail and during four public meetings.
Photo by USFWS

Lake area, the Refuge opted to establish a public waterfowl hunting program during 2005-2006 through a separate planning process, independently of this CCP. All comments, issues, concerns, and opportunities compiled by the Service are summarized in the following narrative which has been organized by several broad topics.

Management

Several meeting attendees observed that the future of Refuge wildlife will rely on establishing sanctuary areas separate from visitor use areas, or establishing times within use areas when wildlife are not disturbed. They asked that visitor uses be compatible with Refuge conservation purposes and that management decisions be based on resource values. One group asked the Service to assess the negative impacts of waterfowl management on other native plants and animals and asked the Service to mitigate the impacts of recreational activities. The same group also requested that the Service assess the effects of predator management strategies to protect sensitive, threatened and endangered species. Some hope to see Refuge staff work with the city of Elk Grove and Cosumnes River Preserve to develop an open space greenbelt to contain development.

A number asked about the Refuge land acquisition priorities and plans for potential acquisitions, hoping to see site specific plans developed for each property that is purchased. Others felt the Refuge needs more conservation easements and other land protection strategies. Specific reference was made to the areas east of Interstate-5 and North of Hood-Franklin Road and also South of Lambert Road as places to favor easements over fee title acquisition.

Some local landowners would like to see a balance between historic land uses, such as agriculture, and expanded recreation opportunities. They suggested that the Refuge establish a 500-foot buffer zone for agricultural spraying and other historic farming activities to avoid problems between existing arming activities and Refuge activities and between privately owned lands and Refuge restoration activities.

There were several comments about the Refuge's floodplain location, the need to maintain its floodplain capabilities and concern regarding how proposed activities and landscape modifications would impact flooding. Refuge plans should leave room for Sacramento County or the State to deal with the Morrison Creek flood problem. They should also recognize that surrounding agricultural lands are on higher ground, providing a natural escape for animals during flooding. Because one of the Refuge's goals is to expand or enhance threatened and endangered species, some neighboring landowners feel they need an incidental take provision that would allow them to continue their farming operations should flooding and endangered species displacement occur.

Along the same lines, concern was expressed about mosquito-related problems and the existing MOU with the Sacramento-Yolo Mosquito and Vector Control District. If an emergency occurs and action is required, there is concern that the bureaucracy will cause unnecessary delays that could impact neighboring private lands. They would like to see some sort of pre-approved plan established for such emergencies.

Some people commented that the Refuge must be a good neighbor and responsible landowner and help pay overhead costs, just as other private landowners. This means that the Refuge should pay water usage fees to the North Delta Water Agency and reclamation districts and pay mosquito abatement costs and other fees. Some feel this has been a source of frustration for ten years and that private landowners cannot subsidize public ownership

A few people asked how the Refuge acquires water rights. One attendee suggested that the Refuge should use treated wastewater because a pipe conveying treated water already passes through the Refuge. People would like to see water quality and groundwater monitored/tested. They would also like assurance that Elk Grove and Sacramento meet clean water standards before their runoff reaches the Refuge. An additional concern regarding waterways relates to the spread of water hyacinth (*Eichhornia crassipes*). A request was made for the Refuge to continue its cooperative program to manage/control water hyacinth and other noxious weeds.

There was a general recognition that Refuge management is labor intensive and that it

should be a high priority for the Refuge to have adequate staffing and funding. A suggestion was made to charge day use fees for all activities to help cover management, expansion, fish stocking, etc.

The Delta Protection Commission acknowledged the Refuge's outreach efforts to invite comments during the CCP process. The Commission's comment reflected their mission of keeping as much land in private ownership as is possible within the primary zone of the Delta and working with the habitat values associated with agriculture. The Refuge Staff was also extended an invitation to brief the Commission about CCP progress.

General Access

Many comments expressed concern about the current lack of, or very limited access to the Refuge. There were numerous requests that the Refuge allow many more types of recreational activities and that these expanded opportunities occur soon.

Many types of recreational uses were mentioned. Hunting received the greatest number of requests, from both individuals and hunting organizations. Horseback riders and a water ski group have accessed portions of the Refuge from private lands since prior to its establishment and they asked for continued access. Comments asked for many other types of uses, including fishing, photography, hiking, birdwatching, small boat launching facilities, bicycle trails, dog trials, environmental education, wildlife observation areas and facilities, picnic and day use facilities and a visitor center. They also requested restrooms. They suggested that the Refuge may want to consider camping or rustic lodging facilities.

Some said that the Refuge should obtain the needed funding to fully staff daily operations to allow improved open access. Several meeting attendees expressed the belief that since this is Federal land, it is their right to have opportunities for these activities. And several offered to support these activities by helping to build facilities, patrol the Refuge, or perform other needed work.

Several comments asked that recreational uses be balanced, specifically requesting that hunting be balanced with other uses. They asked that recreational opportunities be allowed in a way that protects wildlife. They suggested that some activities, such as hunting and wildlife viewing, be restricted to specific areas or times to avoid conflicts.

To support their requests, several made comparisons to Yolo Basin Wildlife Area, observing that it originally had less land under management but supported more types and amount of usage, and to the American River Parkway, which allows considerable recreational usage. They suggested thinking about obtaining funding from other sources for these types of programs. A few attendees hoped that the Refuge would remain rustic and unimproved, calling this "symbolic."

Many asked questions about or commented on the waterways as part of the public trust. They wanted to know if the Refuge's waterways were considered navigable and what the Refuge policy would be regarding their use. Historic use of waterways was cited several times, as well as the belief that use of waterways should not be restricted.

Boating/Waterskiing

Several comments asked that the Refuge provide opportunities for sculling, canoeing, and non-motorized boating or boating with trolling motors only; they also requested a ban on jetskis.

Comments fell on both sides of whether to allow waterskiing. Some felt it was inappropriate. Several members of the local water ski club that has used Beach Lake for many years asked the Refuge to allow this historic use to continue, citing that it is a very seasonal, limited use and does not conflict with other uses or wildlife. They suggested creating a designated waterski area. Several waterskiers offered to help the Refuge by picking up trash or acting as docents of the waterways.

The California Canoe and Kayak School, a paddling school and retail center in

Northern California, asked if there would be an opportunity to open a commercial operation with docent led activities.

Horseback Riding

Several horseback riders who had accessed the Refuge through the privately owned Beach Lake Stables said there has been historical, "prescriptive" use of the Refuge for horseback riding since 1970. They would like to continue to ride on the Refuge, saying that there are only ten to 15 regular riders who ride seasonally.

Some horseback riders attending the meetings asked that the Refuge be opened to riding, with designated areas for riding and other uses. They commented that riding is low impact and can coexist with wildlife and the six priority visitor uses. They would like the opportunity to show it is compatible and requested restrictions on horseback riding if there is a conflict with hunting. Several riders spoke of their willingness to respect the sensitivity of the ecosystem and remain on trails. They offered to organize a volunteer horse patrol, similar to the Folsom Lake patrol and help maintain trails and report poachers, vandalism, fires, etc.

Others expressed concern as to whether horseback riding and hunting would be compatible with each other. One commenter was concerned about the environmental effects of horseback riding, particularly erosion.

Fishing

Several comments asked about the Refuge's plans regarding fishing. Some said they used to fish at Stone Lakes prior to its designation as a national wildlife refuge and would like the opportunity again. They would like year-round fishing, especially bass fishing.

Comments suggested that fishing and hunting should be separated to avoid conflicts. One comment was that if hunting and fishing are allowed, the hunt area should be closed to fishing on hunt days. Another comment suggested that the Refuge should stock fish to provide good family experiences. The Refuge offers a great opportunity for reintroduction of Sacramento perch.

Hunting

There is strong support for a hunting program that includes waterfowl and upland birds, including pheasant, dove, and quail. Many people mentioned that hunting has occurred historically at Lodi Gun Club and other parts of the Refuge both to support their request and as rationale for allowing interim hunting on some of these existing Refuge properties. A few attendees asked to include big game hunting, such as deer (with a shotgun) and small game, such as rabbit.

They also pointed out that hunting exists on other refuges. They feel that if the top third of the Refuge is closed to hunting due to County regulations and the bottom third is closed due to agricultural use, then the middle area south of Hood-Franklin Road should be developed for hunting, not as wildlife sanctuaries. They asked whether hunting could be allowed on the State and County properties that the Refuge manages.

Several specifically requested that the Refuge establish an interim compatibility determination to allow hunting now. A few felt that a hunting program should be developed when suitable property and adequate staffing are available.

In terms of access, some feel that nonconsumptive uses, such as wildlife viewing and photography, are being given and will continue to be given precedence over hunting and fishing. They would like to see a balanced program between hunting and non-hunting areas.

Several asked how the Refuge will manage hunting. Some suggested that the Refuge explore how the California Department of Fish and Game (DFG) manages hunting at other Central Valley refuges. They wondered if there is a general agreement between DFG and the Service, or if each refuge establishes their own arrangement.

Several attendees said that hunting is sustainable and supported by numerous

organizations. Hunting related purchases can help local businesses. Hunters have a long tradition of helping with conservation, funding and facilities. There were numerous references to fees hunters pay to acquire and manage habitat through the Duck Stamp and Federal excise taxes on hunting equipment. Several want to see if some of these funds could be earmarked for a hunting program or to purchase land for hunting at Stone Lakes. They feel the Refuge should expand wetlands and increase ponds available for hunting. There were offers from many hunters to help fund, develop, build and monitor hunting facilities. There were requests that the Refuge develop interpretive materials explaining the role of hunters in conservation.

A number of people expressed concern over a hunting program. A few mentioned hunting related accidents as a cause for concern. Some moved to the area to get away from places that allow hunting and are opposed to it on the Refuge. They would like to see the Refuge advance, but not at the expense of wildlife. They questioned whether hunting is compatible with conservation goals and other uses, such as education and wildlife viewing. They felt that if it is allowed, hunting should not occur at the same time as these other uses. One group was opposed to both hunting and trapping on the Refuge.

Conversely, some said they bought property close to the Refuge because of the potential public access and the prospect of being able to hunt close to home. Many look to the Stone Lakes Refuge as the potential sole opportunity for public hunting in Sacramento County. They want a place where they can hunt locally, without having to drive a long distance. They expressed a need for a hunting program for hunters who do not belong to a duck club.

Others were concerned whether there are adequate bird populations to support observations and hunting and whether hunting causes too much disturbance.

Hunters expressed their hope that the Refuge would not be like Cosumnes River

Preserve, which they feel promised hunting programs and has failed to provide them.

There was strong consensus on developing a junior hunt program; some suggested it could be supported by volunteers with dogs, time and experience. Several people said that a Refuge hunting program should not be just exclusively for junior hunters. It should also be for adult hunters, both beginners and experienced.

The Refuge received many suggestions regarding the proportion of land to be used for hunting, but most felt that from 40 to 50 percent of the Refuge should be hunted. There was strong interest in splitting access between free roam and blind hunting, including floating blinds and two to four person blinds. There were many requests to carefully locate hunt and sanctuary areas. Blinds should be accessible to those with disabilities.

People also had suggestions regarding how hunting access should occur. Some felt that the Refuge should use a lottery/ reservation system and both monitor and limit the number of hunters to assure a quality hunt. Many cited hunting programs at Sacramento, Colusa, Delevan and Gray Lodge as models. They would like to see adequate facilities, such as good land and water access with boat ramps, parking, restrooms and other amenities. A request was made to allow hunting from scull boats and to provide boats to hunters who do no have them.

One commenter was concerned that the Refuge would serve as a sanctuary and draw birds from Yolo (Bypass), negatively affecting hunting in Yolo.

Education/Interpretation

Numerous people commented on the value of the Refuge's educational resources. Several programs were noted, such as school field trips, events and special projects at local schools. Some felt that the primary focus of use for the Refuge should be educational. They would like to see more education programs, including college level

research projects. The Refuge should work with teachers to develop a curriculum and teacher/docent training to enhance the Refuge visitation experience. It should also have a field trip coordinator.

The current limited access and Refuge facilities were noted. Comments asked that the Refuge develop trails and facilities for family use and school field trips. A visitor center and signs along trails would help students learn about the unique features of the Refuge. Having greater access to more areas of the Refuge would allow more community involvement. The Refuge should also consider other outreach sites and centers and do what it can to keep these activities free.

Several visitor improvements were suggested, from a visitor center to new interpretive trails. It was suggested that the money for these improvements would not likely come from Refuge funding, but from private fundraising efforts and other organizations.

Wildlife Observation

Several comments supported wildlife viewing, but stated that the priority must be to maintain habitat for wildlife. The Refuge should control access to prevent an impact on wildlife. They also want to be sure that there are no conflicts between wildlife observation, hunting and other uses.

There were several requests for more trails, good interpretive signing and specific suggestions regarding auto tour routes. The Vic Fazio Yolo Basin Wildlife Area auto tour route was cited as an example for avoiding congestion.

An observation was made that birdwatching lacks a funding base. Birdwatchers should pay a use fee to help cover the costs of facilities. A suggestion was made to see if money from DFG fines could be used to build Refuge facilities.

A specific comment was made that the State Railroad Museum is considering an excursion train for wildlife viewing between the museum and Hood-Franklin Road. We should consider a cooperative venture with them where our interests overlap.

Other Comments

Comments requested other forms of recreational access, such as areas for gun dog training and field trials, bicycle access on existing roads and trapping fur bearing mammals to help reduce the need for a predator control program.

General

A comment was made that the waterways need docents to serve as an extra set of eyes. Two comments were very supportive of the expansion of open space land held by public trust agencies and organizations. This is particularly so for projects involving natural and native habitats, restoration and preservation.

Resource issues and opportunities were also identified during the scoping process. The results of this effort are described in Chapter 4, Problems and Opportunities.

3 Refuge Resources

Ecoregion Setting

Stone Lakes National Wildlife Refuge is located in the Central Valley/San Francisco Bay Ecoregion. This Ecoregion encompasses the Sacramento-San Joaquin Delta located within the San Francisco Bay-Delta Watershed, with an estuary that encompasses roughly 1,600 square miles and drains more then 60,000 square miles of California's runoff (SFEP 2000). The Delta is composed of 57 leveed islands and over 700 miles of sloughs (DWR 2006). The Delta includes the confluence of the two longest rivers in California, the Sacramento and San Joaquin rivers. Following winter rains and Sierra snow melt, the Sacramento River and its tributaries would historically rise above the natural levees and inundate the floodplain. This system was dynamic, depositing rich alluvium, creating and cutting streambanks, providing conditions necessary the growth of riparian forests, changing the river's course and creating oxbow lakes and backwaters, clearing debris and streambeds, exposing and depositing gravel and sand, and creating salmonid spawning habitat. Toward the Delta, with the greater influx of sediment, more substantial natural levees were deposited where larger, more diverse riparian forests occurred (Katibah 1984).

Flyway Setting

The Refuge is located within the Pacific Flyway. The Pacific Flyway is used by millions of waterfowl and shorebirds for migration to wintering and breeding grounds. This Refuge is an important stopover area for migrating shorebirds in the fall and spring and provides important wintering habitat for waterfowl, supporting approximately 60 percent of the total population (CVJV 1990).

Natural/Historic Conditions

Historically the Central Valley supported about four million acres of wetlands with associated grasslands and riparian areas (CVJV 1990). Permanent and seasonal wetlands provided wintering and breeding habitat for waterbirds and other wildlife that flourished through the region. Prior to large scale disturbance, natural processes dominated the area. The Stone Lakes Basin is located within the 100-year floodplain. Historically, periodic floods would sweep through the area changing the course of the rivers and waterways and resetting natural community succession in the area. In addition, fire was a regular component of the area's ecosystem, sweeping through the area every three years.

The 1992 EIS (USFWS 1992) identified the location and extent of historic wetlands in the Refuge planning area, based on U.S. Geological Survey (USGS) atlas sheets of the Sacramento Valley surveyed in 1903-1910. Before 1903, activities related to flood control, water conveyance, and agricultural conversion had already reduced the extent of wetlands prior to the survey. The NRCS, formerly the Soil Conservation Service, mapped locations of hydric soils in 1990 that are generally assumed to correspond to the locations of historic wetlands.

Most of the open water, wetland, and riparian areas present on the Refuge in 1910 have since been drained and converted to agricultural uses. Today, over 95 percent of the riparian habitat in the Central Valley has been destroyed due to agricultural expansion and urbanization. Beach Lake and its associated wetland and riparian vegetation covered a much larger area before it was drained and farmed as recently as the 1960s (Figure 4) (USFWS 1992).

North Stone Lake, which is similar in size to its historic extent, had been drained, cleared and farmed prior to World War II. South Stone Lake was originally about three times its present size extending well west of the former Southern Pacific Railroad levee that now forms its western boundary.

An extensive area of freshwater wetlands 1.0 - 1.5 miles wide, was present in overflow areas east of Snodgrass Slough and between Snodgrass Slough and the Mokelumne River. Bear Lake, a narrow lake more than two miles long located between Lambert Road, Twin Cities Road, Snodgrass Slough and the railroad, no longer exists.

Overflow areas of the Cosumnes River supported extensive freshwater wetlands, about 1 mile wide, upstream of Grizzly Slough and downstream of Twin Cities Road. An unnamed lake about 1.5 miles long and 1,000 feet wide located east of Bruceville and west of the Cosumnes River, was drained and converted to agricultural land.

Little historical data is available that describes waterfowl use of the Refuge. However, maps of the Refuge developed by USGS prior to 1910 indicate that large, tidally influenced, permanent and seasonal wetlands existed, especially in the southern portion of the Refuge toward the Cosumnes River and at Beach, North Stone and South Stone lakes. These wetlands undoubtedly attracted large numbers of swans, geese, ducks and other waterbirds. Levee construction and channelization of rivers, creeks and other natural drainages and conversion of floodplains to agriculture have largely reduced the numbers of breeding and wintering waterfowl the Refuge can support. Historically, ducks were likely more abundant on the Refuge than they are at present (USFWS 1992). Local residents reported successful private duck hunting at South Stone Lake and the farmlands near Hood-Franklin and Lambert Roads from the 1940s until the early 1960s (USFWS 1992). Duck hunting at South Stone Lake was marginal by the early 1960s and has continued to decline during the last three decades (USFWS 1992).

Geographic and Physical Setting
Topography
The Refuge is part of a fairly level, but undulating, ancient alluvial plain incised by Morrison Creek, the Cosumnes River and several small creeks. Morrison Creek traverses the northern portion of the Refuge. The land slopes west to the Sacramento River. Elevations on the Refuge range from near mean sea level to 25 feet above mean sea level. Several small creeks traverse the western and northwestern portions of the Refuge.

While much of the Refuge was laser leveled in the past for agriculture, portions of it, particularly in the North Stone Lake area, still have their native undulating topography.

Geology
The Refuge is within the Great Valley Physiographic Province. The dominant geologic structure is the northwest to southeast-trending asymmetrical syncline that underlies the valley. A syncline is a fold in the rocks of the Earth's crust in which the layers or beds dip inwards, thus forming a trough like structure with a sag in the middle.

The Refuge is underlain by materials comprised of quaternary alluvial and intertidal depositions. Most of the Refuge is underlain by the Victor formation. The Victor alluvial formation was deposited in the late Pleistocene (about one million years ago) by materials washed from the Sierra Nevada. During the mid-Holocene era, about 5,000 years ago, basin, intertidal, levee and channel deposits accumulated along the Sacramento and Cosumnes rivers. The Victor formation consists of poorly sorted alluvial materials that vary in size from clays to boulders. Erosion of the Victor Formation has led to accumulation of finer grained basin deposits along the Sacramento and Cosumnes rivers near the Delta. Intertidal deposits of soft mud and peat accumulated west of Snodgrass Slough at the margin of the Delta. More recently, natural levee and channel deposits have accumulated along the Sacramento and Cosumnes rivers.

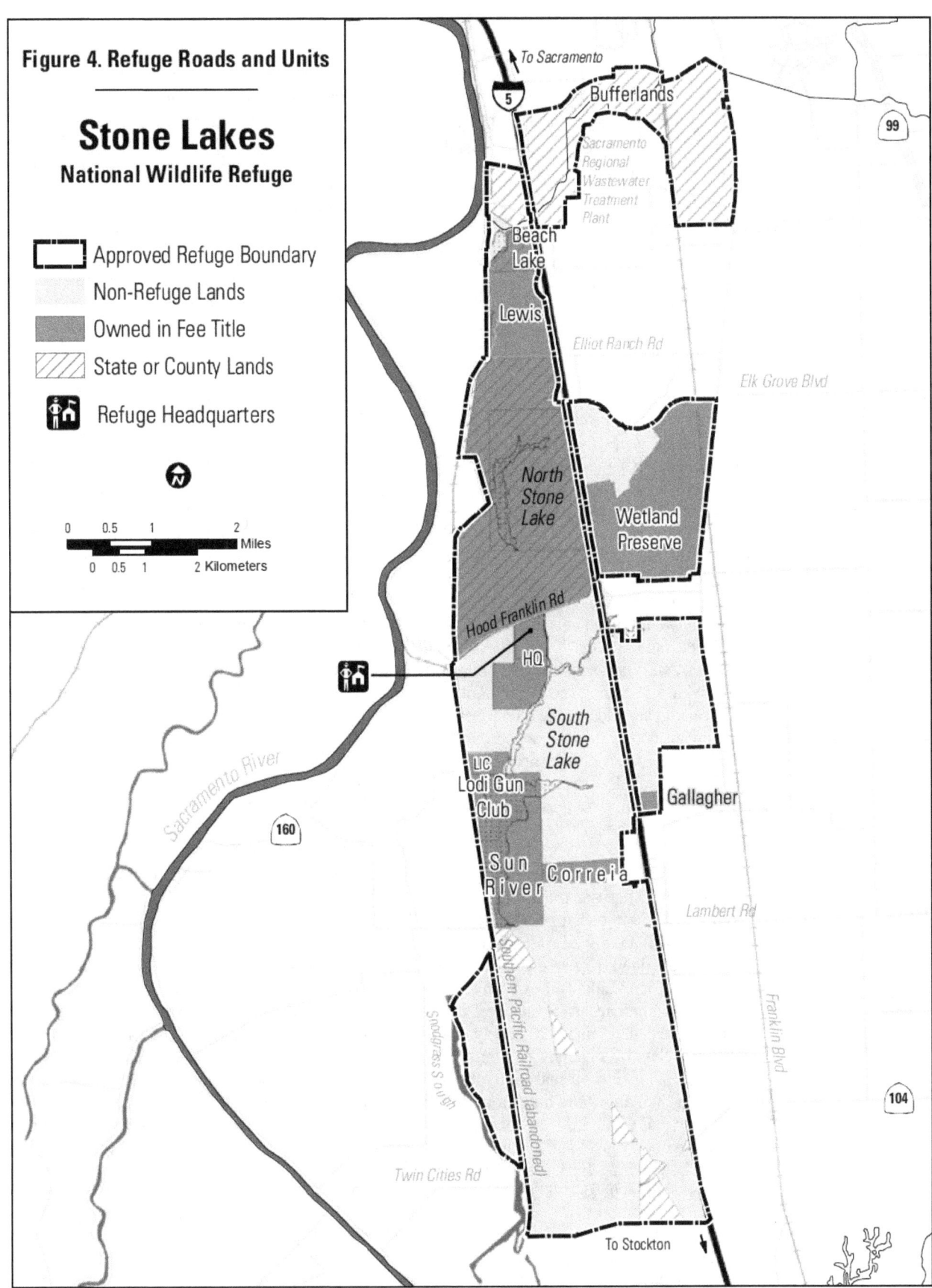

Figure 4. Refuge Roads and Units

Stone Lakes
National Wildlife Refuge

Approved Refuge Boundary
Non-Refuge Lands
Owned in Fee Title
State or County Lands
Refuge Headquarters

0   0.5   1   2
Miles
0   0.5   1   2 Kilometers

To Sacramento

5

Bufferlands

99

Sacramento
Regional
Wastewater
Treatment
Plant

Beach
Lake

Lewis

Elliot Ranch Rd

Elk Grove Blvd

North
Stone
Lake

Wetland
Preserve

Hood Franklin Rd

HQ

South
Stone
Lake

Sacramento River

160

LIC
Lodi Gun
Club

Gallagher

Sun
River   Correia

Lambert Rd

Southern Pacific Railroad (abandoned)

Snodgrass Slough

Franklin Blvd

104

Twin Cities Rd

To Stockton

Soils

Two systems are used by the NRCS to describe the Refuge soils: general soil map units and detailed soil series. The general soil map units represent broad patterns of the soil, topographic relief and drainage classes. Typically, each general soil map unit consists of one or more soil series. The general soil map can be used to compare the suitability of large areas for general land use (USFWS 1992). Soil series maps provide the finer level of detail necessary for site specific planning.

Refuge soils can be classified into three general soil types.
• Egbert Clays and Valpac Loams
• Dierssen sandy clay loams and clay loams
• Clear Lake Clays

Along the Sacramento River, the soils are characteristically very deep and nearly level. These soils are in the floodplain and originally supported extensive wetland and riparian habitats. The Egbert-Valpac general soil type forms a continuous one mile wide strip along the Sacramento River and Snodgrass Slough. It is comprised of somewhat poorly drained soils in areas with a high water table either throughout the year or seasonally. Prime farmland soils with high fertility are generally found in Egbert-Valpac general soil units.

The dominant general soil on the Refuge is Dierssen. Dierssen map units are comprised of somewhat poorly drained soils in areas with a perched water table and are moderately deep to deep over a cemented hardpan. Clear Lake soils, which are present in small areas east of the Dierssen soil unit, are also somewhat poorly drained and underlain by a shallow cemented hardpan. They have a seasonally high water table perched above the hardpan. Both the Dierssen and Clear Lake general soil map units are nearly level and are found in basins and on basin rims. Both areas are protected by flood control levees.

Clays are the most dominant soil particle on the Refuge; thus soils tend to be hydric. Hydric soils correspond to historic locations of wetlands and open water bodies, forming under frequent water saturation and the resulting anaerobic soil conditions. Silty and/or sandy soil belts are interspersed and are identifiable by the associated vegetation. Soils on the Refuge have been divided into soil mapping units. A total of 30 soil map units are found on the Refuge. These map units were used in the EIS (USFWS 1992) to predict the best areas for restoration.

Climate

The Refuge lies between the Coast and Diablo Ranges to the west and the Sierra Nevada to the east. The Carquinez Strait provides a sea-level gap between the Coast Ranges and the Diablo Range. The Carquinez Strait is about 55 miles southwest of the Refuge and the intervening terrain is mainly flat with rolling hills. The prevailing winds blow from the south, primarily due to marine breezes through the Carquinez Strait. During winter, the sea breezes diminish and winds from the north occur more frequently. However, winds from the south still predominate. The climate in the Refuge area is temperate and semiarid, with hot, dry summers and cool, damp winters. Annual temperatures in the area average highs of 52 degrees Fahrenheit in January to about 93 degrees Fahrenheit in July and lows of 38 degrees Fahrenheit in January to 58 degrees Fahrenheit in July. Annual precipitation averages about 17 inches. Dense "tule" fog is common in winter (USFWS 1992).

Air Quality

Air Pollution Control Agencies. The Federal Clean Air Act (42 U.S.C. §§ 7401, as amended) mandates the establishment of ambient air quality standards and requires areas that violate these standards to prepare and implement plans to achieve the standards by certain deadlines. The deadline for attaining both the ozone and carbon monoxide (CO) standards was August 31, 1988. Areas that do not meet Federal primary air quality standards are designated as "nonattainment" areas. Areas that comply with Federal air quality standards are designated as "attainment" areas. Attainment and nonattainment designations are pollutant specific. Thus, while Sacramento County is a nonattainment area for particulate matter less than 10 microns in diameter (PM10) and ozone it is an attainment area for carbon monoxide (CO), nitrogen oxide (NO_x), sulfur dioxide (SO_2) and lead.

Many agencies are involved in air pollution control, including the U.S. Environmental Protection Agency (USEPA 2006), California Air Resources Board (ARB), Sacramento Metropolitan Air Quality Management District (SMAQMD) and other air quality management districts (AQMDs).

In California, all agricultural burning is regulated jointly by the ARB and local AQMDs. Each day the ARB determines, based on recent and anticipated weather conditions, whether the following day will be a permissible burn day or a no-burn day. Each ARB's primary objective in making this determination is to control the amount of smoke from agricultural burning that reaches urban areas. On permissible burn days, few restrictions are placed on the amount of land that may be burned in the region. On no-burn days, fields may be burned only if a special permit has been issued by the local AQMD. Such burn permits are allocated based on an estimated allowable acreage for the entire region.

Ambient Air Quality Standards and Existing Air Quality in Sacramento County

Both the State of California and the Federal government have established a variety of ambient air quality standards. The following discussion focuses on the ambient standards and existing concentrations for PM10, ozone and CO for two reasons: Sacramento County's air quality currently exceeds the allowable ambient standards for PM10 and ozone and these pollutants, together with CO, are the primary pollutants that could be affected by the Refuge.

PM10. Health concerns associated with suspended particles focus on those particles small enough to reach the lungs when inhaled. Few particles larger than

10 microns in diameter reach the lungs. Consequently, both the Federal and State air quality standards for particulate matter have been recently revised to apply only to these small particles (designated as PM10).

The entire Sacramento Valley, including Sacramento County, is classified as a PM10 moderate nonattainment area (USEPA 2006). Both the 24 hour and annual California PM10 standards are violated on a regular basis in the Sacramento area (USFWS 1992). Sacramento County PM10 emissions are generated by a variety of sources, primarily entrained road dust, construction and demolition activities. Farming operations and agricultural waste burning are also important sources of PM10 in Sacramento County.

Ozone. Ozone is a respiratory irritant that also increases susceptibility to respiratory infections. Ozone causes substantial damage to leaf tissues of crops, natural vegetation and damages many materials by acting as a chemical oxidizing agent.

The Federal air quality standard for ozone is exceeded several times a year at monitoring stations in Sacramento County. As a consequence of the recorded violations of the Federal ozone standard, the entire Sacramento Valley Air Basin, including Sacramento County, has been designated a serious nonattainment area of ozone (USEPA 2006). This indicates that the ozone levels in the Sacramento Valley air basin are a potential threat to public health. Human health effects of ozone can include difficulty breathing and lung tissue damage (ARB 2006).

Ozone, the main component of photochemical smog, is primarily a summer and fall pollution problem. Ozone is not emitted directly into the air but is formed through a complex series of chemical reactions involving other compounds that are directly emitted. These directly emitted pollutants, also known as ozone precursors, include reactive organic gases (ROG) and NO_x (ARB 2006). The period required for ozone formation allows the reacting compounds to be spread over a large area, producing a regional pollution problem. Ozone problems are the cumulative result of regional development patterns, rather than the result of a few significant emission sources. Motor vehicles are the primary source of NOx and ROG in Sacramento County and therefore, are primary contributors to regional ozone concentrations.

Carbon Monoxide (CO). CO combines readily with hemoglobin and thus reduces the amount of oxygen transported in the bloodstream. Relatively low concentrations of CO can meaningfully affect the amount of oxygen in the bloodstream because CO binds to hemoglobin 220-245 times more strongly than oxygen. Both the cardiovascular system and the central nervous system can be affected when 2.5 percent to 4.0 percent of the hemoglobin in the bloodstream is bound to CO rather than to oxygen. State and Federal ambient air quality standards for CO have been set at levels intended to keep CO from combining with more than 1.5 percent of the blood's hemoglobin (U.S. EPA 1978, California ARB 1982).

Sacramento County has been designated as a nonattainment area for CO in the past, but is no longer considered a nonattainment area (USEPA 2006). Motor vehicle emissions are the dominant source of CO in most areas. As a directly emitted pollutant, CO disperses as it is transported away from the emission source, reducing pollutant concentration. Consequently, CO problems are usually localized, often the result of a combination of high traffic volumes and traffic congestion. Data from previous studies suggest that CO problems occur primarily near major traffic arteries having large amounts of commercial development. The Refuge is located on either side of Interstate-5 adjacent to and within the Sacramento urban area.

CO is primarily a winter problem. High CO levels develop primarily during winter when periods of light winds or calm conditions combine with the formation of ground level temperature inversions (typically in the evening through early morning period). These conditions result in reduced dispersion of vehicle emissions, allowing CO problems to develop and persist during hours when traffic volumes are declining from peak levels. It is unknown how elevated CO levels affect Refuge resources. Motor vehicles also exhibit increased CO emission rates at low air temperatures (USFWS 1992).

Contaminants and Water Quality

Water sources within the Refuge boundary include Morrison and Laguna creeks, Upper and Lower Beach lakes, urban runoff and agricultural drainage, Southern Pacific Cut (SP Cut), North and South Stone lakes and groundwater. Water quality monitoring by the SRCSD and the Service have been completed to date on the Refuge and in the surrounding area.

Water quality in North and South Stone Lakes is affected by limited Delta and San Joaquin River daily tidal flows moving up Snodgrass Slough through the Lambert Road bridge water control structure. Agricultural activities upstream of lakes may influence water quality from direct drainage into the lakes and the SP Cut. Groundwater discharge/recharge and Mokelumne River upflow via Snodgrass Slough to and from the lakes may also influence water quality in the lakes. The SRWTP does not discharge effluent into the Morrison Creek watershed. Instead, the treated effluent is dechlorinated and discharged directly to the Sacramento River near the community of Freeport.

The Refuge has many drainages that originate in urban and agricultural areas and empty into Refuge wetlands and lakes. In addition, a significant portion of land within the approved Refuge boundary is currently in agriculture. These areas are likely sources of nonpoint source contaminants, however they also provide important habitat for fish, aquatic invertebrates and foraging areas for birds that feed on these resources. Monitoring of aquatic habitats for nonpoint pollution is important, especially on this Refuge which is surrounded by urban development and actively managed agriculture.

The Sacramento Regional Wastewater Treatment Plant conducts ongoing quarterly water sampling for certain trace elements at several locations along Morrison Creek, Laguna Creek, and Meadowlark and Black Crown lakes. Furthermore, the USACE sampled water from the Morrison Creek watershed from 1982 to 1984. Concentrations of cadmium (Cd), copper (Cu) and lead (Pb) exceeded the USEPA acute toxicity criterion for aquatic life in all samples. The DFG and SWRCB collected and analyzed largemouth bass (*Micropterus salmoides*) from Meadowlark Lake from 1985 – 1987 and analyzed for heavy metals and organochlorine pesticides (OCs). Elevated levels of mercury (Hg), Cu, chlordane, dacthal, total DDT and total polychlorinated biphenyls (PCBs) were detected. Environmental contaminants are clearly present in the Stone Lakes area, but have been poorly delineated.

Baseline sampling on the Refuge and in nearby areas was conducted by the Service in 1997. The Service collected water, sediments, crayfish, fish, and waterbird eggs and analyzed them for OCs, PCBs and trace elements. Generally low levels of trace elements were found in water and biota, and generally low levels of organic compounds were present in sediments and biota. Concentrations of certain trace elements exceeded the USEPA's threshold effects level in sediments. Concentrations of trace elements were consistently higher (relative to other sites) in sediments from Lower Beach Lake. Lower Beach Lake is the terminus of Morrison Creek and may accumulate contaminants that originate in the greater Sacramento metropolitan area. Further sampling and toxicity tests of water and sediments are needed to identify the source of the contamination in Lower Beach Lake and other nearby areas (USFWS 2003a).

Water, sediment and biota samples were collected from eight locations (three sites in Morrison Creek, two sites in North Stone Lake and three sites in South Stone Lake) in spring on 1997 (Thomas 1997). Samples were analyzed for dissolved oxygen, temperature, heavy metals (arsenic, cadmium, copper, lead, mercury, selenium and zinc), salts (sodium chloride, calcium ion and magnesium), Nitrate NO_3 and pH. Results indicate that levels of heavy metals, although present, were not sufficient to cause deleterious impacts to wildlife; concentrations of selenium in all five waterbodies tested are above levels recommended for the protection of aquatic life.

Additional sampling was conducted from December 1998 to January 2000 on stormwater runoff onto the Refuge. The water quality of the Refuge and surrounding areas is continuously being degraded by irrigation drainwater and urban drainage in the summer, and the flushing of accumulated pollutants via urban stormwater runoff in the winter. Water samples and water quality data (temperature, dissolved oxygen, conductivity and pH) were collected from 11 sites on the Refuge during four storm events from December 1998 to January 2000. Temperature, pH, dissolved oxygen and conductivity were within normal limits for all sites, except for dissolved oxygen at Morrison Creek, which was at or below 3.0 milligrams/liter (mg/L) during two of the storm events. Overall, trace element concentrations in stormwater entering the Refuge were relatively low. Seven of 16 trace element samples collected during the two storm events had copper concentrations above the hardness adjusted chronic criterion and of those, three were also above the acute criterion. Four of 16 samples had lead concentrations above chronic criterion. Only one sample out of 16 had a concentration of cadmium that would be considered significantly elevated above the hardness adjusted chronic criterion (3.75 times the criterion). Nearly all sites had Diazinon levels above DFG's proposed 50 mg/L chronic criterion; however, they did not all produce measurable toxicity when daphne (*Ceriodaphnia dubia*) were exposed to the samples. Two sites, one on the Lower Beach Lake Unit and another that flows into Lower Beach Lake, consistently showed levels of Diazinon that produced toxicity to *Ceriodaphnia* along with detectable levels of chlorpyrifos. Concentrations of Diazinon at these sites ranged from 101 to 1,488 mg/L with measured toxicity units ranging from 3.2 to 3.5 (USFWS 2003b).

Sacramento County's National Pollutant Discharge Elimination System (NPDES) Municipal Permit requires that pollutants found in urban stormwater runoff be reduced to the maximum extent possible. Dry detention stormwater runoff treatment facilities were constructed as part of the 3,000-acre development east of the Refuge identified in the East Franklin Specific Plan and would likely be included in other projects as well. These detention basins are effective in reducing pollutants by 30 to 90 percent.

Discharge Water Quality Monitoring
The Central Valley Regional Water Quality Control Board (Regional Board) issued order No. R5-2006-0054, regulating discharges from irrigated lands, effective beginning July 1, 2006 and ending June 30, 2011 (CVRWQCB-CVR 2006). The order detailed an individual discharger conditional waiver of waste discharge requirements. The order states that individual dischargers can seek coverage under the Individual Discharger Conditional Waiver or under the Coalition Group Conditional Waiver, by joining a coalition group. The conditional waiver requires Dischargers to pay a fee to the State Water Board. The Water Quality Control Plan for the Central Valley Region designates beneficial uses and establishes water quality objectives (CRWQCB-CVR 2004).

During the development of the irrigated lands waiver the Regional Board included discharges from "managed wetlands" in the definition of irrigated lands (USFWS 2004). However, the term "managed wetlands" is not defined by the Regional Board. There is a broad range of management activities that occur on Refuge wetlands. Some forms of management are relatively passive while others are very intensive due to enhance habitat for endangered and threatened species as well as migratory birds.

During the development of the waiver, the Service objected to being included under the waiver and recommended that a separate waiver be developed for managed wetlands. The Regional Board recognized that wetland discharges were sufficiently different than agriculture and a separate waiver would be appropriate but they did not have sufficient funds and staff to develop a separate waiver at the time. Thus the Regional Board's irrigated lands waiver and its requisite monitoring programs are primarily designed to address pesticide discharges from agriculture and does not take into consideration the differences and uniqueness of wetlands.

Meeting the waiver requirements is at best awkward for wetland managers, including the Refuge, because the irrigated lands waiver is designed to address discharges from irrigated agriculture. In evaluating the irrigated lands waiver requirements, the Service believes that the monitoring requirements for an individual discharger under the waiver are more appropriate for wetland discharges. They require monitoring of pesticides and toxicity only if certain chemicals or pollutants of concern are discharged, whereas the primary monitoring program for coalitions requires monitoring of all pollutants of concern since a coalition is more likely to represent a large variety of pesticide uses and discharge types.

The Refuge manages seasonal and permanent wetlands on the South Stone Lake, Headquarters and Beach Lake Units totaling approximately 335 acres. Periodic draw downs of the permanent wetland impoundments on the Lewis and Beach Lake units are done when vegetation, such as cattails, covers more than 75 percent of the wetland and to control weeds and undesirable fish species, such as carp. During years with no restrictions on water use, flood ups of seasonal wetlands begin in early to mid-September and continue through late fall depending on rainfall. Drawdowns commence in early April and continue through mid-June. Seasonal wetland drawdowns are accomplished through a combination of evaporation and opening of water control structures. Depending on annual rainfall, flood waters are pumped out of the Sun River property of the South Stone Lake Unit to minimize damage to infrastructure and facilitate draw downs. Supplemental summer irrigation of seasonal wetlands to stimulate desirable plant growth for migrating waterfowl is done in late July and early August to a maximum depth of 12 inches for 24 hours and then drawndown by opening water control structures within a few days.

Only one type of discharge to waters of the State, as defined in Regional Board order No. R5-2006-0054, occurs on the Refuge: storm water runoff from the Refuge during flooding events. Discharge to waters of the State is defined by order No. R5-2006-0054 as "Surface discharges, such as irrigation return flows, tailwater, drainage water, subsurface drainage generated by irrigating crop land or by installing and operating drainage systems to lower the water table below irrigated lands (tile drains), stormwater runoff flowing from irrigated lands, stormwater runoff conveyed in channels or canals resulting from the discharge from irrigated lands, and/or operational spills containing waste" (CVRWQCB-CVR 2006). See "Current Management Practices: Wetlands" in Chapter 3 for a detailed discussion of Refuge wetland management practices.

Pesticide Use and Toxicity Testing
The Service does not propose to do toxicity testing of its wetland discharges. All pesticide use on the Refuge, is part of an Integrated Pest Management (IPM) plan and adheres to pesticide label instructions, Intra-Service Section 7 Consultations under the Endangered Species Act, Sacramento County pesticide bulletin protective measures for threatened and endangered species, buffer requirements and other appropriate best management practices.

Since the mid-1990s, the Refuge has collaborated with a number of private, local and state entities as a participant in the Stone Lakes Basin Water Hyacinth Control Group (SLBWHCG). As a result of water hyacinth control efforts to date, the extent of plant infestations has been reduced to an estimated 30 to 35 acres. With continued applications, it is anticipated that beyond 2006, control efforts may be scaled back to occasional treatments (two to three per week) during the hyacinth growing season to spot-treat small infestations.

The Stone Lakes Basin water hyacinth control program is permitted under a Statewide National Pollution Discharge Elimination System (NPDES) General Permit (No. CAG990005) for discharge of aquatic pesticides. Field crews with the Service and the SRCSD conduct chemical control of water hyacinth on approximately 670 acres of open water habitats on Lower Beach Lake, SP CUT (the borrow channel for the former Southern Pacific Railroad), North Stone Lake and South Stone Lake and its tributaries. Control activities occur in natural lakes and sloughs as well as man-made irrigation or drainage ditches and channels. Treated waterways lie within lands owned by the Service, the State of California, Sacramento County and a number of private landowners. Since infestations of water hyacinth within the Basin have been greatly reduced due to past efforts, it is anticipated that a steadily decreasing quantity of herbicide will be needed as the program becomes more of a maintenance operation. To comply with the monitoring and reporting requirements of the NPDES General Permit, the Refuge and SRCSD provide an annual report to the California Regional Water Quality Control Board summarizing aquatic pesticide applications and the results of water quality monitoring for the water hyacinth control program.

The Refuge also cooperates with Sacramento-Yolo Mosquito Vector Control District (SYMVCD) to mitigate the risk of mosquito borne diseases. See Appendix A, Compatibility Determination for Monitoring and Control of Mosquitos for detailed information. The SYMVCD and the Service rely on a full range of IPM techniques to manage mosquito populations, including wetland design features, water and vegetation management, biological control and chemical control of larval or adult mosquitos. As a result of IPM practices larvicide applications on the Refuge have been limited to small acreages and adulticides have historically been used infrequently (i.e., three ground ultra-low volume applications during 10 years). Largely due to the 2005 detection of West Nile Virus, the Refuge received ground ultra-low volume applications of the adulticide pyrethrin on 18 occasions in 2005 and six applications to date in 2006. Additional applications of adulticides are likely during the remainder of the 2006 season. .

Since the majority of Refuge uplands are not irrigated they do not technically fall under the irrigated lands waiver. The IPM methods that the Refuge uses to control weeds include burning, mowing, discing and application of herbicides including Roundup (glyphosphate) and 2, 4-D. Multiple treatments on the same acreage in one year are rare and are usually spot applications. Also, since these are Refuge uplands, virtually all areas where applications occur have vegetated buffers between applications and any waterbodies.

While irrigated agriculture is conducted within the approved Refuge boundary, it is not conducted on lands under the control (i.e., fee title ownership, cooperative management agreement, conservation easement) of the Refuge. While participating in a watershed monitoring coalition group with adjacent irrigated agricultural producers is a possible option, discharge from adjacent agricultural lands is ultimately the responsibility of the discharger.

The Refuge, by policy and mandate, is managed utilizing many of the best management practices to reduce pesticide and fertilizer runoff, they are considered the basic elements of good refuge habitat management. Refuge policy mandates limited use of pesticides only after physical or other means (e.g., controlled burns,

grazing, mowing) are used and after review and approval by management. Most herbicide treatments are a part of long-term habitat restoration and management plans on uplands where treated areas are being restored to native habitat. Except for approximately 490 acres of irrigated pastureland, Refuge uplands are not irrigated.

All applications of herbicides on Refuge uplands occur where there are natural vegetated buffers from aquatic habitats. Many riparian areas have understory vegetation that minimizes potential drift into waterbodies. Also, aerial applications are not utilized on the Refuge. Applications for upland weeds are typically spot treatments of discrete stands of plants and multiple applications on the same acreage in one year are rare . For these reasons the Service does not propose to do toxicity testing of its wetland discharges.

Pesticide Monitoring

The Refuge and SRCSD will continue monitoring of water quality required under the NPDES General Permit for the application of aquatic herbicides for the water hyacinth control program. Given that minimal discharge, if any, occurs from the Refuge and that water quality monitoring is already occurring, the Refuge intends to file as an individual discharger, under the Central Valley Regional Water Quality Control Board's, Irrigated Lands Conditional Waiver for water dischargers.

Water Quality is further discussed in Chapter 4.

Hydrology

The Refuge lies within the Beach-Stone Lakes Basin in the northeast portion of the Sacramento-San Joaquin Delta. This Basin is within the lower watershed of the Morrison Creek drainage, with the Sacramento River to the west and the Mokelumne and Cosumnes rivers nearby to the southeast (Figure 1). The lower Morrison Creek watershed governs the surface water flow patterns over the Refuge. This 180-square-mile system of streams and floodplain originates in eastern Sacramento County and includes portions of the City of Sacramento, Morrison, Unionhouse, Laguna, Elk Grove and Elder creeks. Streamflows in these channels are affected by storm runoff, springs, urban drainage, groundwater pumping for irrigation, water supply and diversions and surface storage ponds located throughout the watershed. Waters on the Refuge are also influenced by the Cosumnes and Mokelumne rivers, especially during floods when water from the two rivers backs up the Southern Pacific Railroad borrow canal (SP Cut).

The Morrison Creek stream group drains a large urban and agricultural watershed that includes Laguna and, Morrison creeks and Beach Lake. Many commercial and industrial sources contribute runoff to Morrison Creek. Most streams are intermittent and historically dry during the summer. Today, urbanization and agricultural practices in this watershed have resulted in low summer flows consisting of runoff from irrigation, wastewater flows and agricultural return flows (USFWS 1992).

Elevations in the Morrison Creek watershed range from 300 feet above mean sea level (MSL) in the northeast and slope gently down to sea level in the Beach-Stone Lakes Basin in the southwest. Construction of a reclamation district levee before the turn of the century divides Upper Beach Lake, which extends northeastward under Interstate-5, from Lower Beach Lake. This levee directs water draining down Morrison Creek from Upper Beach Lake to an electric pump (City Sump 90) that discharges it directly into the Sacramento River near the town of Freeport.

During winter high-flow periods when Upper Beach Lake rises 3 feet above MSL, water overtops the dike dividing Upper and Lower Beach Lake and spills into Lower Beach Lake and the Southern Pacific railroad borrow ditch (SP Cut). Water then continues south to North Stone Lake, Hood-Franklin Road and South Stone Lake; passes through the Lambert Road Bridge flood control structure; and then enters Snodgrass Slough. Snodgrass Slough provides a surface hydrologic connection for the Basin and the Sacramento-San Joaquin Delta near the town of Locke (Jones and Stokes Associates 1989). Nearly all the lands within the approved Refuge boundary are within the 100-year floodplain.

Also see Chapter 4, Hydrology.

Water Supply

Water sources available for maintenance and management of Refuge fish and wildlife habitats and irrigation include: runoff from local sources such as the Morrison Creek drainage, shallow groundwater and surface flows from Snodgrass Sough. Surface flows from direct precipitation and surplus irrigation returns within the Beach-Stone Lakes Basin provide water sources for habitats and farming operations adjacent to the SP Cut. The Basin and SP Cut are also used as a tailwater and stormwater runoff drain for reclamation districts lying to the west.

Interception of shallow groundwater is used to sustain habitats and agricultural lands within the Refuge and the Beach-Stone Lakes Basin. Due to irrigation withdrawals, there is a groundwater depression in the water table south and east of the Refuge area. This groundwater depression creates a gradient away from the Sacramento River and locally induces flow from the river across the Refuge area toward the center of the depression. Therefore, groundwater that is intercepted by channels and wells within the Beach-Stone Lakes Basin is likely seeping from the river.

In response to the daily tidal cycle, water levels in Snodgrass Slough and the SP Cut are influenced by operation of a slide gate and flap gates on the Lambert Road Bridge flood control structure; diversion of water by various upstream users, including the Refuge and operation of the Delta Cross Channel by the California Department of Water Resources for the State Water Project. South to north flows of surface water occur through the Lambert Road Bridge flood control structure and these reverse flows play a substantial role in sustaining the water supply in the Beach-Stone Lakes Basin.

Biological Resources
Plant Communities

Vegetation communities are categorized below as grassland, riparian, woodland or wetland (Figure 5. Vegetation Map). Agricultural crops, vineyards, and urban developments are only addressed on the Vegetation Map.

Grasslands. Grasslands on the Refuge are broken into three categories: annual grassland, perennial grassland and irrigated pastures. Grasslands are open habitats supporting grasses and forbs with little or no woody vegetation. The gently rolling terrain surrounding North Stone Lake is covered with large areas of annual grasslands mixed with seasonal wetlands.

Annual. Most of the grasslands in California are dominated by annual, nonnative grasses and forbs as a result of cultivation, livestock grazing, changes in fire regimes and other disturbances (Heady 1988). Characteristic species include the dominant species, wild rye (*Elymus* spp.), as well as wild oats (*Avena fatua*), bromes (*Bromus* spp.) and filarees (*Erodium* spp.). Some annual grasslands are interspersed with native perennial grasses and forbs. Restoration and management are a focal part of grassland management for native grasses and forbs, such as creeping wild rye and California poppy (*Eschscholzia californica*), as well as many other species. The grazing regime is the primary tool, used by managers, to enhance native grassland species; however, prescribed burning (see Appendix D. Fire Management Plan), water manipulations, mowing and discing are also utilized. See the section on "Grasslands" under "Current Management" later in this chapter for more information.

Perennial. Before Euroamerican settlement, most of the Central Valley grassland was dominated by native purple needlegrass (*Nassella pulchra*). Open areas between the tussocks of this perennial bunchgrass supported many wildflowers, including owl's clover (*Orthocarpus purpurascens*), lupine (*Lupinus* spp.), brodiaea (*Brodiaea* spp.) and many others. This native grassland community, known as valley needlegrass grassland, has been almost completely replaced by annual grassland. Remnants of valley needlegrass grassland occur as small patches, usually in marginal habitats, such as undisturbed moist sites and areas protected from grazing or only lightly grazed. Valley needlegrass grassland may occur on the Refuge, although no occurrence has been identified. Another native perennial grassland that was once common is the valley wild rye grassland, dominated by creeping wild rye and associated with California mugwort (*Artemisia* spp.) and stinging nettle (*Urtica dioica*). Patches of this grassland occur on the Refuge and are being actively restored.

Irrigated Pasture. Irrigated pastures on the Refuge are irrigated and optimally grazed in the summer months (June through August) to promote and enhance native vegetation. Grazing is monitored to provide a mosaic of habitats, thus increasing biodiversity. Monitoring consists of visual calibration and measuring residual dry matter in pounds per acre. These pastures support a good ratio of forbs (eg., clovers, lupines, poppies and succulent grasses) to grasses, which provide valuable forage for white-faced ibis (*Plegadis chihi*), geese, black-bellied plovers (*Pluvialis squatarola*) and others. Currently, irrigated pastures, found on the North Stone Lakes and Gallagher properties, play a valuable role in habitat and wildlife management.

Grassland Wildlife. Grassland habitats are important foraging areas for many species. Less than 1 percent of California's native grassland remains due mainly to advances in large-scale irrigation in the 1930s; therefore, grassland management plays a vital role in contributing to the Refuge System's biological integrity, diversity and environmental health. Refuge grassland management promotes grasslands at varying heights and densities in order to create a mosaic of grassland habitats at the

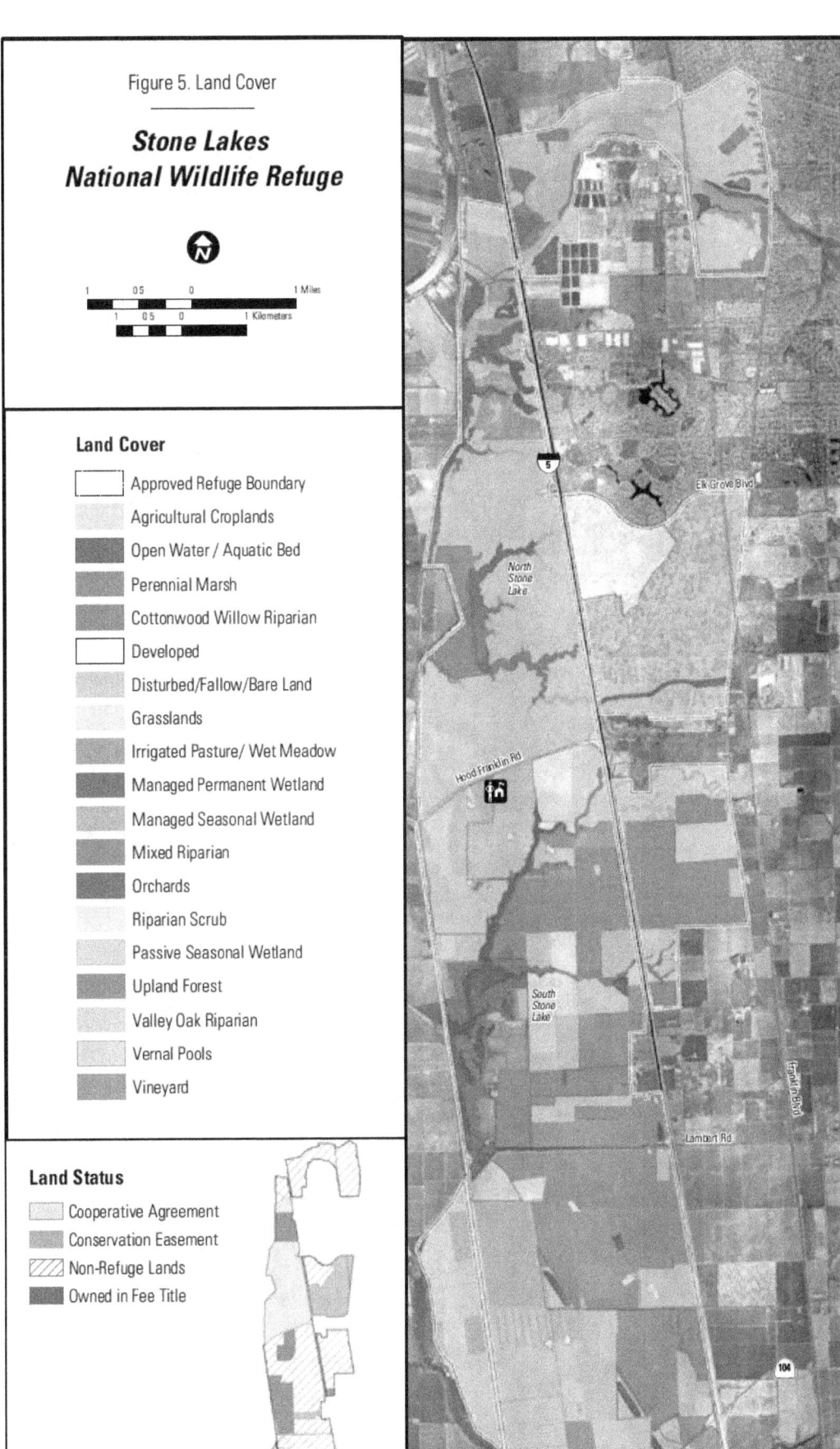

Figure 5. Land Cover

Stone Lakes
National Wildlife Refuge

1 0.5 0 1 Miles
1 0.5 0 1 Kilometers

Land Cover

Approved Refuge Boundary
Agricultural Croplands
Open Water / Aquatic Bed
Perennial Marsh
Cottonwood Willow Riparian
Developed
Disturbed/Fallow/Bare Land
Grasslands
Irrigated Pasture/ Wet Meadow
Managed Permanent Wetland
Managed Seasonal Wetland
Mixed Riparian
Orchards
Riparian Scrub
Passive Seasonal Wetland
Upland Forest
Valley Oak Riparian
Vernal Pools
Vineyard

Land Status

Cooperative Agreement
Conservation Easement
Non-Refuge Lands
Owned in Fee Title

ecosystem level. Species utilizing grasslands dominated by shorter grasses include birds of prey such as northern harriers (*Circus cyaneus*), white-tailed kites (*Elanus leucurus*), red-shouldered hawks (*Buteo lineatus*) and Swainson's hawks; shorebirds such as the black-bellied plover; wading birds such as white-faced ibis, great blue herons (*Ardea herodias*) and great egrets (*Ardea alba*); tree swallows (*Tachycineta bicolor*), cliff swallows (*Petrochelidon pyrrhonota*), barn swallows (*Hirundo rustica*) and other species of birds. Species utilizing taller grass habitats include savannah and white-crowned sparrows (*Passerculus sandwichensis, Zonotrichia leucophrys*) , western meadowlarks (*Sturnella neglecta*), California horned larks (*Eremophila alpestris*), loggerhead shrikes (*Lanius ludovicianus*) as well as mammals such as coyote (*Canis latrans*), deer mice (*Peromyscus maniculatus*), pocket gophers (*Thomomys bottae*), black tailed hares (*Lepus californicus*), California voles (*Microtus californicus*) and California ground squirrels (*Spermophilus beecheyi*). Since species often utilize more than one habitat type, the aforementioned habitats and their associated species are generalizations.

Riparian Forest. Riparian forests support the densest and most diverse wildlife communities in the Sacramento Valley. The diversity of plant species and growth forms provide a variety of food and microhabitat conditions for wildlife. The unique combination of surface water and groundwater, fertile soils, high nutrient availability and layered vegetation provide diverse conditions for wildlife. North and South Stone Lakes support riparian scrub and forest habitats along with marshes dominated by cattail (*Typha* sp.), tule (*Schoenoplectus acutus* var. *occidentalis*), smartweed (*Polygonum* sp.) and season wetlands. Riparian habitat is also supported along some of the ephemeral swales and stream courses found in the Refuge.

Riparian areas are particularly important to migratory wildlife as they provide corridors along migration routes. It is important to maintain the integrity and continuity of riparian corridors which provide nesting and foraging habitat and shelter from inclement weather and predation. For these reasons, riparian restoration and management is a vital part of the Refuge's habitat and wildlife management. Three types of riparian forests occur on the Refuge: cottonwood, mixed, and valley oak (*Quercus lobata*). Mature riparian forests are diverse, multilayered communities associated with occasional to frequent flooding and perennial subsurface water.

Cottonwood Riparian Forest. Cottonwood riparian forests occur along perennial streams where inundation occurs every spring. The forest canopy is dominated by Fremont cottonwood (*Populus fremontii*) and Goodding's willow (*Salix gooddingii*) typically draped with California grape vines (*Vitis californica*). The understory often supports California box elder (*Acer negundo* var. *californicum*), California blackberry (*Rubus ursinus*), white-stemmed raspberry (*Rubus leucodermis*), buttonbush (*Cephalanthus occidentalis*) and blue elderberry (*Sambucus mexicana*).

Mixed Riparian Forest. Mixed riparian forests occur in areas where the floodwater inundation occurs more often and for longer periods of time than valley oak and less often

Riparian forests support the densest and most diverse wildlife communities in the Sacramento Valley.
Photo by USFWS

and for shorter duration than cottonwood. Canopy dominants include Fremont cottonwood, valley oak, Goodding's willow, red willow (*Salix laevigata*), yellow willow (*Salix lucida*), California black walnut (*Juglans hindsii*) and California sycamore (*Platanus racemosa*). Common understory dominants include California box elder, Oregon ash (*Fraxinus latifolia*), poison oak (*Toxicodendron diversilobum*) and buttonbush. California grape envelops trees and shrubs in this area, giving this forest a jungle-like appearance.

Valley Oak Riparian Forest. The highest portion of the floodplain with the least frequent inundation supports the valley oak riparian forest. Valley oak riparian forest persists in well-drained soils which are not extensive within the Refuge boundary. The dense forest canopy is dominated by valley oak with associated tree species of Oregon ash, California sycamore, and California black walnut. The understory typically supports annual grasses, however, moister soils support vines and shrubs, such as poison oak, California blackberry and wild rose (*Rosa californica*).

Valley Oak Woodland. Scattered valley oaks form woodland and savanna habitats on deep, well-drained alluvial soils. Typically the valley oak is the only tree found in this community. The understory is usually annual grassland, but moister sites support shrubs, such as poison oak and wild rose. Valley oak woodland is often transitional between valley oak riparian forest and valley oak savanna. Valley oak woodlands are not prominent on the Refuge because of a lack of appropriate soils and elevations to support their growth; however, valley oak woodland can be found on the Lewis Unit.

Wetlands. Two wetland vegetation types occur on the Refuge: perennial and seasonal. Seasonal vegetation can be divided into two categories, vernal pools and seasonal vegetation in actively managed wetland units or cells. Refuge wetlands are managed to maintain and enhance biodiversity, particularly for waterbirds, reptiles, amphibians and invertebrates. North

The highest portion of the floodplain with the least frequent inundation supports valley oak dominated riparian forest, shown being restored above with the active support of volunteers from the Sacramento Tree Foundation.
Photo by USFWS

and South Stone Lakes support wetlands dominated by cattail, tule and smartweed along with seasonal wetlands. The most extensive areas of freshwater marsh and aquatic bed vegetations in southern Sacramento County are at South Stone Lake.

Perennial. Shallow, perennial wetland vegetation consists primarily of cattails, tules, cottonwood, willow, sedges (*Carex* spp.) and rushes (*Juncus* spp., *Scirpus* spp.). The vegetation varies in regards to the presence of tules and cattails, both of which require more saturated conditions than most seasonal wetlands provide. Conversely, wetlands also vary in regards to watergrass (*Echinochloa crus-galli*), swamp timothy (*Crypsis schoenoides*) and annual smartweed (indicative of seasonal wetlands), which require seasonal irrigation, as opposed to frequent or constant inundation.

Seasonal. Seasonal wetland vegetation on the Refuge is usually considered transitional between perennial wetlands and vernal pools. Seasonal wetland vegetation consists primarily of watergrass, swamp timothy, annual smartweed, curly dock (*Rumex crispus*), cocklebur (*Xanthium strumarium*), sedges and rushes. Seasonal wetlands are managed to promote vegetation that has relatively higher food

The most extensive areas of freshwater marsh and aquatic bed vegetations in southern Sacramento County are at South Stone Lake, on the Refuge.
Photo by USFWS

value for migratory waterbirds, as well as to provide cover and substrate for birds, mammals, reptiles, amphibians and invertebrates.

Vernal Pools. Vernal pools are ephemeral or seasonal shallow pools with an underlying impervious layer. The pools fill with rain water in the winter and retain water through the spring until they evaporate due to the Central Valley's intense summer heat. There are over 150 plant species associated with similar vernal pool habitat on the nearby Cosumnes River Preserve and 90 percent of the plants are native with more than half of them being endemic. Plants and animals associated with vernal pools are adapted to the unique environment of vernal pools. For example, orcutt grasses (*Orcuttia* spp.) have a submergent vegetative phase with floating leaves. As the pools dry, a terrestrial phase emerges. Typical vernal pool species include downingia (*Downingia* spp.), Sacramento and pilose orcutt grass (*Orcuttia viscida, Orcuttia pilosa*), popcorn flower (*Plagiobothrys* spp.), goldfield (*Lasthenia* spp.), vernal pool tadpole shrimp (*Lepidurus packardi*), fairy shrimp (*Branchinecta lynchi*), California tiger salamander (*Ambystoma californiense*), western toad (*Bufo boreas*) and the western spadefoot toad (*Spea hammondii*), although some of these species can also be found in some of the seasonal wetland units. The majority (98 percent) of the Refuge vernal pools can be found on the Wetland Preserve Unit, with the rest found on the Lewis Unit. Barely 12 percent of the vernal pools located on the Refuge are naturally occurring; the remainder have been created over the last 14 years as mitigation for vernal pool

losses due to development. The Wetland Preserve Unit is owned in fee title by AKT Development Corporation and managed by the Refuge under a conservation easement.

Cattle grazing and prescribed fire are the primary management tools for maintaining and enhancing vernal pools with grazing considered most beneficial for vernal pool plants, invertebrates and amphibians (J. Marty, TNC, pers. comm.). Primary benefits of grazing come from phytomass removal and trampling of nonnative invasive annual grasses and other weeds in the pool margins and surrounding uplands. If left unchecked, these non-native plant species competitively exclude native vernal pool plants, especially around pool margins; reduce the inundation period of the pool which increases evapotranspiration; promote the grow of algae, which appears to negatively affect vernal pool crustaceans; and can inhibit the overland migration of vernal pool-breeding amphibians (Robins 2002). In addition to discouraging nonnative grasses, cattle also compact the soil to where grazed vernal pools hold water an average of 50 days longer than un-grazed vernal pools. This enhanced water retention capability also provides benefits for plant and wildlife species. The Wetland Preserve Unit of the Refuge is managed by the Service under conservation easement. Refuge staff are in the process of developing a grazing management plan in cooperation with the landowner that will protect vernal pool and other seasonal wetland habitats on the unit.

Wildlife
The diverse vegetation of the Beach-Stone Lakes Basin provides habitat for a range of mammals, birds, reptiles, amphibians and invertebrates. Wildlife can be found on all units of the Refuge. North and South Stone Lakes are especially important wildlife habitat areas because of the combination of grasslands, extensive riparian forest, seasonal and perennial wetlands and open water they support. A survey of North Stone Lake reported sightings of three amphibian species, eight reptile species, 101 bird species and 23 mammal species (USFWS 1992). The same survey also

reported finding active nesting sites of 52 great egrets, 49 great blue herons, 61 black-crowned night-herons (*Nycticorax nycticorax*), 20 snowy egrets (*Egretta thula*), and 17 double-crested cormorants (*Phalacrocorax auritus*).

South Stone Lake is rich in riparian and wetland habitats supporting a diversity of amphibian, reptile, bird and mammal species. Two waterfowl hunt clubs were operated on the lake for many years prior to establishment as a refuge. However, hunting success has declined substantially during the last three decades. The primary waterfowl species likely to be encountered at South Stone Lake are mallard (*Anas platyrhynchos*), American wigeon (*Anas americana*), green-winged teal (*Anas crecca*) and occasionally, northern pintail (USFWS 1992).

Mammals. Grassland habitats support small prey species, such as deer mice, California voles, pocket gophers, California ground squirrels, desert cottontails (*Sylvilagus auduboni*) and black-tailed hares. Ungrazed grasslands with dense cover typically support more wildlife species than do grazed pastures or disturbed grasslands and some species prefer ungrazed pastures, such as badgers (*Taxidea taxus*), black-tailed hares, coyotes and California ground squirrels.

Valley oak woodlands supply acorns for western gray squirrels (*Sciurus griseus*) and black tailed deer (*Odocoileus hemionus*), which depend on the acorns as a critical autumn food source. Riparian forest and scrub provide habitats for many of the same species as the valley oak woodlands. Mature cottonwood, Goodding's willow and valley oak trees provide habitat for cavity-nesting species, such as bats, western gray squirrels, raccoons (*Procyon lotor*) and ringtails (*Bassariscus astutus*). Riparian understory plants, such as California grape, blackberry and elderberry, supply food sources for Virginia opossum (*Didelphis virginiana*), raccoon, striped skunk (*Mephitis mephitis*) and gray fox (*Urocyon cinereoargenteus*). As with birds, narrow

and discontinuous riparian areas favor wildlife that forage near, in or over water, such as beavers (*Castor canadensisis*), river otters (*Lutra canadensis*) and bats. Riparian scrub provides cover and forage for California ground squirrels. Beavers preferentially feed on young cottonwood shoots and many small mammals feed on willow seeds. Bramble thickets offer escape cover to desert cottontails and black-tailed hares. Aquatic areas near riparian scrub habitats provide foraging habitats for carnivores and omnivores, such as river otters and gray foxes. Ground insectivores that inhabit riparian scrub include broad-footed moles (*Scapanus latimanus*). Striped skunks also prey on other small animals using the riparian scrub.

Perennial wetlands support river otters, muskrats (*Ondatra zibethicus*) and beavers. Upland species, such as black-tailed hares and desert cottontails, take cover and forage at the margins of wetland habitats.

Birds. Over 200 bird species have been sighted at in the Beach-Stone Lakes Basin (USFWS 2003a). About 90 species are confirmed to have nested on the Refuge. These species include numerous waterbirds, songbirds, and raptors. For a detailed list of birds see Appendix E.

Refuge grasslands are important foraging areas for many birds of prey, such as black-shouldered (white-tailed) kites, red-tailed hawks (*Buteo jamaicensis*), Swainson's hawks, red-shouldered hawks, northern harriers, golden eagles (*Aquila chrysaetos*), American kestrels (*Falco sparverius*), prairie falcons (*Falco mexicanus*), great horned owls (*Bubo virginianus*) and barn owls (*Tyto alba*). Songbirds forage in grassland habitats, including loggerhead shrikes, yellow-billed magpies (*Pica nuttalli*), horned larks, water pipits (*Anthus rubescens*), western bluebirds (*Sialia mexicana*), savannah sparrows and a variety of swallow species. A few birds nest in grasslands, such as killdeer (*Charadrius vociferous*), ring-necked pheasants (*Phasianus colchicus*), northern harriers, western kingbirds (*Tyrannus*

The mature Fremont cottonwood, willow (*Salix* spp.) and valley oak trees of riparian vegetation provide nesting support for large birds, such as hawks, owls, American crows (*Corvus brachyrhynchos*), great egrets and great blue herons. Cavity nesting birds, such as woodpecker species and wood ducks (*Aix sponsa*), require mature stands. Dense understory consisting of blackberry (*Rubus* spp.), raspberry (*Rubus* spp.),

verticalis) and western meadowlarks. Ungrazed grasslands with dense cover typically support more wildlife species than do grazed pastures or disturbed grasslands. However, some bird species prefer grazed pastures, such as burrowing owls (*Athene cunicularia*), mourning doves (*Zenaida macroura*), Brewer's blackbirds (*Euphagus cyanocephalus*), turkey vultures (*Cathartes aura*), red-tailed hawks, black-shouldered kites, ring-necked pheasants and yellow-billed magpies. Pastures on the Refuge and nearby farmland may represent an important stopover point for geese during spring migration; more than 1,500 white-fronted geese (*Anser albifrons*) were observed on pasture near Hood-Franklin Road in the late 1970s (USFWS 1992) and large numbers continue to use grasslands adjacent to North Stone Lake. Canada (*Branta canadensis*), snow (*Chen caerulescens*) and Ross' (*Chen rossii*) geese are also observed on Refuge pastures and waterbodies regularly during spring. Except for some species such as robins, blackbirds, and mourning doves, vineyards provide virtually no suitable bird habitat, while orchards can provide some nesting habitat for birds of prey and food and cover for other birds and mammals.

California grape and elderberry produce important food for wildlife. Common birds that depend on the nectar, fruits, and seeds of riparian plants include California towhees (*Pipilo crissalis*), spotted towhees (*Pipilo maculatus*), Anna's hummingbirds (*Calypte anna*) and black-headed grosbeaks (*Pheucticus melanocephalus*).

The high quality riparian vegetation on the Refuge provides excellent habitat for neotropical migrants. The riparian and valley oak woodland vegetation supports an abundance of insect prey that sustain a high diversity and density of migratory and resident birds, including western flycatchers (*Empidonax difficilis*), yellow warblers (*Dendroica petechia*), MacGillivray's warblers (*Oporornis tolmiei*) and song sparrows (*Melospiza melodia*). Habitat destruction and nest parasitism by nonnative brown-headed cowbirds (*Molothrus ater*) may be primary causes of bird decline on the Refuge (USFWS 1992). Insectivorous species that have dramatically declined or been eliminated from the Central Valley's nesting avifauna, but have been seen on the Refuge, include: yellow-billed cuckoos (*Coccyzus americanus*), willow flycatchers (*Empidonax* spp.), yellow warblers, yellow-breasted chats (*Icteria virens*) and blue grosbeaks (*Passerina caerulea*). Some riparian areas are narrow and discontinuous and favor wildlife species that forage in adjacent grassland or agricultural fields, including black-shouldered kites, American kestrels and western kingbirds. Riparian areas also provide perches and cover for species that forage in or over water, such as double-crested cormorants, green-backed herons (*Butorides virescens*), belted kingfishers (*Ceryle alcyon*), black phoebes (*Sayornis nigricans*) and violet-green swallows (*Tachycineta thalassina*). Riparian scrub provides cover and forage for California (valley) quail (*Callipepla californica*), ring-necked pheasants, American goldfinches (*Carduelis tristis*), lesser goldfinches (*Carduelis psaltria*) and California towhees. Bramble thickets provide potential nesting habitat for tri-colored blackbirds (*Agelaius tricolor*). Aquatic areas near riparian scrub habitats provide foraging habitats for ground insectivores, such as killdeer, spotted sandpipers (*Actitis macularius*) and western kingbirds.

Valley oak woodlands provide shade, shelter and nesting habitat for many bird species, including various woodpecker species and other cavity-nesting birds, such as American kestrels, western screech owls (*Megascops kennicottii*), white-breasted nuthatches (*Sitta carolinensis*) and western bluebirds. Acorns are an important food source for many species, including acorn woodpeckers (*Melanerpes formicivorus*), valley quail, northern flickers (*Colaptes auratus*) and scrub jays (*Aphelocoma californica*). Valley oak foliage and bark attract insects that are eaten by ash-throated flycatchers (*Myiarchus cinerascens*), plain titmice (*Baeolophus inornatus*), white-breasted nuthatches and northern orioles (*Icterus galbula*). Valley oak woodlands provide the best habitat on the Refuge for aerial-foraging species, such as acorn woodpeckers, ash-throated flycatchers and western wood-pewees (*Contopus sordidulus*). This habitat also offers perch sites for ground foraging species, such as western bluebirds

and northern flickers. Swainson's hawks, red-tailed hawks and black-shouldered kites use valley oak woodlands as habitat because they require sturdy nesting sites with open canopy for easy access. Great blue heron and great egret maintain important rookeries in the valley oak woodlands near North Stone Lake and near Black Crown Lake on the Bufferlands Unit.

Perennial wetlands provide habitat for a variety of species, including pied-billed grebe (*Podilymbus podiceps*), American bitterns (*Botaurus lentiginosus*), American coots (*Fulica Americana*) and Virginia rails (*Rallus limicola*). Upland species, such as ring-necked pheasants and California quail, take cover and forage at the margins of wetland habitats. Diving and dabbling ducks and other aquatic birds also use the perennial wetlands of North and South Stone Lakes and the Bufferlands; however, most wintering waterbirds depend on the seasonal wetlands.

Waterbirds that make extensive use of the managed wetlands at North Stone Lake and the Bufferlands include grebes, herons, egrets, pelicans, cormorants, rails, cranes, plovers and other waterbird species (USFWS 1992). Flooded pastures and croplands and other seasonal wetlands provide foraging and roosting habitat for thousands of shorebirds migrating along the Pacific Flyway. For example, 4,090 shorebirds and 4,440 waterbirds were observed at Upper Beach Lake in a single survey on April 28, 1990 (USFWS 1992). A DFG aerial survey conducted in February 1972 recorded 5,750 waterfowl in the Beach-Stone Lakes basin. As many as 15,000 waterfowl were observed on other surveys (USFWS 1992). Dominant waterfowl species included tundra swans (*Cygnus columbianus*), snow geese, white-fronted geese, Canada geese, mallards, northern pintails, northern shovelers (*Anas clypeata*), cinnamon teal (*Anas cyanoptera*), green-winged teal, wood ducks and ruddy ducks (*Oxyura jamaicensis*). The Service also collected data on waterbird abundance in the Beach-Stone Lakes basin during January through March in 1982 and 1983.

Refuge grassland habitats commonly support reptiles like this rehabilitated gopher snake, shown being released onto the Refuge.
Photo by USFWS

birds forage on submerged aquatic plants and associated invertebrates in aquatic beds associated with open water. Fisheries in open waters of Beach Lake, and North and South Stone Lakes provide an important food source for fish eating species, including American white pelicans (*Pelecanus erythrorhynchos*) and double-crested cormorants. In addition, double-crested cormorants nest at North Stone Lake (USFWS 1992).

Reptiles and Amphibians. Reptiles and amphibians can be found among the various habitat types on the Refuge. Common reptiles and amphibians on the Refuge include Pacific treefrogs (*Hyla regilla*), bullfrogs (*Rana catesbeiana*), western pond turtles (*Clemmys marmorata*), pond slider turtles (*Trachemys scripta*), western fence lizards (*Sceloporus occidentalis*), western terrestrial garter snakes (*Thamnophis elegans elegans*) and gopher snakes (*Pituophis catenifer*). Suitable habitat exists for the federally-threatened giant garter snake along sparsely vegetated lakes, sloughs and wetlands. Refuge grassland habitats commonly support gopher snakes, common garter snakes (*Thamnophis sirtalis*), California kingsnakes (*Lampropeltis getulus californiae*), western fence lizards and western toads. Valley oak woodland reptiles observed at North Stone Lake include western fence lizards, California alligator lizards (*Elgaria multicarinata multicarinata*), western yellow-bellied racers (*Coluber mormon*), Pacific gopher snakes, California kingsnakes and common garter snakes. Amphibians have also been seen in the valley oak woodlands at North Stone Lake, including bullfrogs, western toads and Pacific treefrogs. Reptiles seen in the riparian scrub include the ground insectivorous western fence lizard and the predatory gopher snake. Perennial wetland habitat provides breeding and foraging habitat for common garter snakes, Pacific treefrogs and bullfrogs. This habitat also has the potential to provide habitat for the giant garter snake. When standing water is available, amphibians such as California tiger salamanders, western toads and Pacific

The basin supported two million annual bird use days (one bird present for one day); of these 1.2 million were waterfowl (USFWS 1992). Based on the observations of local landowners and data collected by the Service, DFG and Ducks Unlimited, the Refuge appears to be most important as a feeding and resting area for waterfowl in the early spring rather than an important overwintering area. North and South Stone Lakes have the potential to be managed as waterfowl breeding and nesting areas during the spring and summer (USFWS 1992). Other wetland obligate bird species include common yellowthroats (*Geothlypis trichas*), red-winged blackbirds (*Agelaius phoeniceus*) and marsh wrens (*Cistothorus palustris*).

Open water portions of the Refuge's lakes, ponds and sloughs offer roosting habitat for waterbirds, such as pied-billed grebes, eared grebes (*Podiceps nigricollis*), common moorhens (*Gallinula chloropus*), American coots and a variety of waterfowl species. Diving and dabbling ducks and other water treefrogs use vernal pools for egg laying and for the development of their young.

Fish. Fish are found in all bodies of water on the Refuge, including North and South Stone Lakes. Various surveys done from 1992 to present have yielded 30 species on the Refuge (See Appendix F, Fish List). Only five of the species observed, Sacramento blackfish (*Orthodon microlepidotus*), prickly sculpin (*Cottus asper*), hardhead minnow (*Mylopharodon conocephalus*), California roach (*Hesperoleucus symmetricus*) and sculpin are California natives. Common fish on the Refuge include mosquito fish, threadfin shad (*Dorosoma petenense*), black crappie (*Pomoxis nigromaculatus*), redear sunfish (*Lepomis microlophus*), catfish (*Ictalurus* spp.), largemouth bass, carp (*Cyprinus carpio*) and common bluegill (*Lepomis macrochirus*) (D. Vanicek , CSUS, 1999, B. Treiterer, USFWS, pers. comm.). Other introduced species include silverside (*Menidia beryllina*) and shrimp species. While many problems are associated with introduced fishes, they have a value for sportfishing (largemouth bass, catfish, etc.), controlling mosquitos (*Gambusia* spp.), and as forage for other fish and wildlife.

North and South Stone Lakes are best described as shallow and eutrophic, characterized by enriched dissolved nutrient levels (such as phosphates) that stimulate growth of aquatic plants and algae. As the abundant plants and algae decay the dissolved oxygen levels are reduced by microbial blooms. Due to the abundant plankton, these lakes are dominated by planktivorous (plankton-eating) fish. The food chain is stimulated by nutrients from abundant bird use, which helps produce the dense phytoplankton population. The phytoplankton in turn support a large zooplankton population, which supports the fish. Piscivorous (fish-eating) fish are not abundant in the lakes. The SP cut is less turbid than the lakes and contains fewer planktivorous fish.

Aquatic habitats occurring on the Bufferlands of the SRWTP consist of

Laguna and Morrison creeks and five lakes. A total of 22 fish species have been documented from Bufferlands waterbodies. Meadowlark Lake comprises 19 acres of permanent water and was created as a borrow pit for construction of Interstate-5. It is filled each winter from overflows of Morrison and Laguna creeks and has steep banks with almost no vegetation. Black Crown Lake covers 28 acres and is very similar in nature and origin to Meadowlark Lake. However, it has some vegetation for cover and shade, is connected to Morrison Creek, and has a more stable water level in summer. Nineteen and 21 species of fish have been documented from Meadowlark and Black Crown lakes, respectively. Nicolaus Pond is an 8 acre pond, fed with water from the Captein Dairy and Laguna Creek Fish Farm. The banks are gradual and contain some grassy areas and some emergent vegetation. Five species of fish have been found in this pond. Fishhead Lake was created as part of a wetland mitigation project. The lake consists of 13.5 acres of permanent water with an additional 30.5 acres of seasonal water. Tailwater from Laguna Creek Fish Farm feeds the lake almost year round. The banks are steep, but stable water levels have allowed emergent vegetation to become established. The lake contains 18 species of fish. The 6.2-acre Lost Lake was formed from an abandoned gravel mining operation. Most of the lake is about ten feet deep and steep sided. Five species have been found in Lost Lake.

About 16,000 lineal feet of Laguna Creek passes through the Bufferlands. It is not channelized and appears to be high quality fish habitat. The upper sections have gentle slopes and large patches of emergent vegetation while the lower sections are lined with mature riparian trees. A total of 14 species of fish have been found in the creek. A 15,000 lineal foot section of Morrison Creek runs through the Bufferlands and receives most of its summer water from Sacramento storm drains. Fish kills have been observed here in the past, possibly a consequence of impaired water quality. Above its confluence with Laguna Creek, Morrison Creek is highly channelized and appears to have little high quality fish habitat. Some stretches of bank are vegetated; however, most banks are steep and bare when water levels recede during the summer. In summer, large patches of floating water primrose (*Ludwigia peploides*) sometimes cover the entire surface of the creek. Past the confluence, the banks are lined with riparian trees offering a higher degree of cover. Ten species of fish have been found in Morrison Creek.

Invertebrates. There has been no comprehensive invertebrate survey conducted at the Refuge. However, some surveys occasionally conducted by SYVCMD and refuge staff have found that aquatic vertebrates, such as grass shrimp, Louisiana swamp crayfish, clam shrimp (*Cyzicus californicus*), Odonata larvae (dragon and damselfly), Notonectiday larvae (backswimmers), cladocerans, copepods and water beetles (Corixidae larvae), inhabit seasonal and permanent wetlands and also the vernal pools.

Vernal pools are located on the Wetland Preserve, North Stone Lake and Beach Lake units of the Refuge. Please see the description of vernal pool fairy shrimp and vernal pool tadpole shrimp below. Two species of fairy shrimp, the vernal pool fairy shrimp and the vernal pool tadpole shrimp, have been identified in the pools.

Special Status Species
Stone Lakes provides or has the potential to provide habitat for Federal Endangered Species Act (ESA) and California Endangered Species Act (CESA) threatened and endangered species.

Federally-listed Species
Vernal pool fairy shrimp (*Branchinecta lynchi*). The vernal pool fairy shrimp is an ESA listed threatened species and is a small (0.4 inches to 1.0 inch long) crustacean with a delicate elongate body, large stalked compound eyes and 11 pairs of swimming legs. This species is endemic to vernal pool habitats in California and southwestern Oregon (USFWS 1994).

Vernal pool fairy shrimp typically inhabit vernal pools with clear to tea-colored water, most commonly in grass or mud-bottomed swales, or basalt flow depression pools in unplowed grasslands. They also may exist in alkaline vernal pools. The water in pools inhabited by this species has low total dissolved solids, low conductivity, low alkalinity and low chloride. Fairy shrimp feed on algae, bacteria, protozoa, rotifers and bits of detritus (USFWS 1994).

The primary threats to vernal pool fairy shrimp are the loss and alteration of habitat due to urban and agricultural development and random extinction by virtue of the small isolated nature of the remaining population.

Vernal pools are found on the Wetland Preserve and Lewis Units. Vernal pool fairy shrimp have been documented within vernal pools on the Wetland Preserve Unit.

Vernal pool tadpole shrimp (*Lepidurus packardi*). The vernal pool tadpole shrimp is an ESA listed endangered species. Vernal pool tadpole shrimp are primarily benthic (living on the bottoms of the pools) animals that swim with their legs down. Vernal pool tadpole shrimp climb or scramble over objects, and plow along bottom sediments as they forage for food. Their diet consists of organic detritus and living organisms, such as fairy shrimp and other invertebrates (USFWS 2003c). Females disperse fully developed cysts into the pool, where the cysts are then deposited into the sediment. Vernal pool tadpole shrimp pass the summer months as dormant cysts in the soil. Some of the cysts hatch as the vernal pools are filled with rainwater in the next or subsequent seasons, while other cysts may remain dormant in the soil for many years. When winter rains refill inhabited pools, tadpole shrimp reestablish from dormant cysts and can become sexually mature within three to four weeks of hatching (Ahl 1991; Helm 1998). The tadpole shrimp will continue to grow as long as their vernal pool habitat remains inundated, in some cases for six months or longer. They periodically shed their shells, which can often be found along the edges of vernal pools where vernal pool tadpole shrimp occur. Mature vernal pool tadpole shrimp range from 0.6 to 3.4 inches in length. Mature adults may be present in pools until the habitats dry up in the spring (USFWS 2003c).

Tadpole shrimp can be found in California's Central Valley and the San Francisco Bay area. The geographic range of this species includes disjunct occurrences in the Central Valley, from Shasta County to northern Tulare County and in the Central Coast Range from Solano County to Alameda County. The primary threats to vernal pool tadpole shrimp are the same as for the vernal pool fairy shrimp.

Vernal pools can be found on the Wetland Preserve and Lewis units. Vernal pool tadpole shrimp have been documented within vernal pools on the Wetland Preserve Unit.

Valley elderberry longhorn beetle (*Desmocerus californicus dimorphus*, VELB). The valley elderberry longhorn beetle is an ESA listed threatened species. The VELB is a medium-sized beetle, typically about two cm long.

The VELB is associated with elderberry trees (*Sambucus* spp.) during its entire life cycle. The adults emerge from pupation inside the wood of these trees in the spring as their flowers begin to open. The exit holes made by the emerging adults are distinctive small oval openings. Often these holes are the only detectable clue that the beetles occur in an area. The adults feed on elderberry foliage until about June, when they mate. The females lay eggs in crevices in the bark. Upon hatching, the larvae begin to tunnel into the tree where they will spend one to two years eating the interior wood, which is their sole food source.

The elderberry tree is associated with riparian forests which occur along rivers and streams. Historically the VELB ranged throughout the Central Valley; however, recent surveys have revealed the VELB to persist only in scattered localities along the Sacramento, American, San

Joaquin, Kings, Kaweah and Tule rivers and their tributaries. Over 95 percent of our riparian forests have been cleared in the past century for agricultural, as well as urban and suburban, and development uses (Smithsonian Zoological Park). The wood from these forests has also been used extensively as fuel and building materials. Additionally, extensive use of pesticides, grazing and other mismanagement have severely degraded otherwise undisturbed patches of riparian habitat.

There are no documented sightings of the VELB or of any exit holes on the Refuge. However, elderberry trees of appropriate size can be found on the Lewis Unit. New elderberry shrubs planted for mitigation on the South Stone Lake Unit are expected to reach the appropriate size for VELB habitat in the future.

Giant garter snake (*Thamnophis gigas*). The giant garter snake is an ESA listed threatened species. Historically, the range of this snake was the San Joaquin Valley from the vicinity of Sacramento and Antioch southward to Buena Vista and the Tulare Lake Basin (CDFG 2000). The current distribution extends from near Chico to Fresno County. This species is one of the most aquatic garter snakes and is usually found in areas of freshwater marsh and low gradient streams. Permanent wetlands are especially important as they provide habitat over the summer and early fall when seasonal wetlands are dry. Although the snake is absent from larger rivers (such as the Sacramento River), it has adapted to human made habitats, such as drainage canals and irrigation ditches, especially those associated with rice farming. Riparian woodlands do not provide suitable habitat because of excessive shade and inadequate prey resources (USFWS 1993).

Generally quite aquatic, these garter snakes forage primarily in and along streams, taking fish, amphibians and amphibian larvae (Fitch 1941). Most current food sources may be introduced species, such as carp, mosquito fish, and bullfrogs, because the native prey such as blackfish, thick-tailed chub (*Gila crassicauda*) and red-legged frog (*Rana aurora draytoni*) are no longer available (Rossman et al. 1996). Courtship and mating normally occur soon after spring emergence. Young are born alive between mid-July and early September, usually in secluded sites, such as under the loose bark of rotting logs or in dense vegetation near pond or stream margins.

The giant garter snake is now very scarce throughout its range in the Central Valley. Populations have been eliminated or decimated by the elimination of natural sloughs and marshy areas. Heavy use of pesticides is also suspected as a contributing factor in the decline of this once abundant garter snake. Fortunately, protection of waterfowl habitat may allow it to survive in a small portion of its original range.

The giant garter snake was last documented on the Refuge 14 years ago in 1992 at Beach Lake. The species is presumed to be present throughout the Refuge where suitable habitat exists (Wylie 1997). The Refuge lies within the Sacramento Basin subpopulation of the giant garter snake.

Bald eagle (*Haliaeetus leucocephalus*). The bald eagle has suffered from habitat destruction and degradation, illegal shooting and contamination of its food source, most notably due to the pesticide DDT. The bald eagle is listed as an ESA threatened and CESA endangered species. Although there have been no documented sightings of the bald eagle on the Refuge, (DFG 2004) habitat exists for them on the Refuge.

State-Listed Species
Greater sandhill crane. The greater sandhill crane is a CESA listed threatened species. The Refuge and adjacent public and private lands provide habitat for greater and lesser sandhill (*Grus canadensis canadensis*) cranes. The California Central Valley provides wintering habitat for 6,000 – 6,800 cranes, nearly 14 percent of the world's total population of greater sandhill cranes (Pacific Flyway Council 1997). The San Joaquin-Sacramento Delta is one of the two most important winter use areas for the

Central Valley population of greater sandhill cranes; over 61 percent of the Central Valley population has been recorded on the Delta (Ivey and Herziger 2001).

Historically, greater sandhill cranes were fairly common breeders on California's northeastern plateau (Grinnell and Miller 1944). The greater sandhill crane is now reduced greatly in numbers and breeds only in Siskiyou, Modoc, Lassen, Plumas and Sierra counties (James 1977; Remsen 1978; McCaskie et al. 1979). The subspecies winters primarily in the Sacramento and San Joaquin Valleys (Grinnell and Miller 1944) but can also be found near Brawley in Imperial County and Blythe, in Riverside County (Garrett and Dunn 1981), along with lesser sandhill cranes. Greater sandhill cranes formerly wintered more commonly in Southern California, but have declined greatly there and throughout their range. They are extremely rare outside of their known wintering grounds except while migrating over interior California. There have been a few coastal sightings from Marin County southward, but there are no records from offshore islands.

The Refuge's wintering cranes migrate southward from the northeast in September and October and northward in March and April. Cranes travel in great flocks, both day and night, with stops only for short periods to feed and rest. Migration is rapid and direct. In winter, cranes frequent dry grasslands and croplands especially near open and emergent wetlands (Grinnell and Miller 1944), although they may also feeds on dry plains far from water. When foraging, cranes prefer open treeless short grass plains, grain fields and open wetlands where predators can be easily seen (Grinnell and Miller 1944, Cogswell 1977). They feed mostly on cereal crops (e.g., newly planted or harvested) and will also consume grasses and forbs. Cranes also use their long bills to probe in soil for roots, tubers, seeds, grains, earthworms and insects. Larger prey, such as mice, small birds, snakes, frogs, and crayfish, are also taken (Terres 1980; Eckert and Karalus 1981). Fruits and berries are eaten if available (Eckert and Karalus 1981).

Grazing can be detrimental to sandhill crane, when they are nesting and fledging (Littlefield and Ivey 2002), however nesting is not known to occur on the Refuge.

Cranes roost at night in flocks standing in moist fields or in shallow water (Terres 1980). They also roost in expansive, dry grasslands, island sites, and wide sandbars (Johnsgard 1975; Eckert and Karalus 1981).

In California, sandhill cranes establish nesting territories in wet meadows that are often interspersed with emergent marsh habitat. The last statewide breeding population study in California was conducted in 1988. The breeding population in California was estimated to be 276 pairs. Favorable roost sites and an abundance of cereal grain crops characterize the cranes' preferred Central Valley wintering ground. Rice is used extensively by cranes near the Butte Sink area of Butte County and corn is the principal food source at most other Central Valley wintering areas, particularly in the Sacramento-San Joaquin Delta near Lodi in San Joaquin County. Irrigated pastures are chosen for resting sites throughout the wintering ground. A key requirement of wintering habitat is a communal roost site consisting of an open expanse of shallow water (CDFG 2000).

Currently, the estimate for greater sandhill cranes within their Pacific Flyway range is between 5,000 and 6,000 individuals. This species continues to experience threats on both wintering and breeding grounds by agricultural and residential conversion of habitat, predation, human disturbance and collisions with power lines (CDFG 2000).

Surveys indicate 300-350 greater sandhill cranes feed, roost and loaf on the Refuge during the winter season. The cranes roost and forage in managed impoundments, pastureland, and other agricultural land throughout and adjacent to the Refuge. Cranes are commonly seen on irrigated pastures on the South Stone Lake Unit and on the grasslands of North Stone Lake and the Wetland Preserve Unit. They can also be found on the Whitney (in the southeast

When foraging, greater sandhill cranes prefer open treeless short grass plains, grain fields and open wetlands where predators can be easily seen.
Photo by USFWS

corner) and Zacharias Island properties, lands that are not managed by the Refuge but are within the approved refuge boundary. In general, a mix of greater and lesser sandhill cranes can be found south of Hood-Franklin Road, with only greater sandhill cranes occurring north of Hood-Franklin Road.

Swainson's hawk (*Buteo swainsoni*). The Swainson's hawk is a State-listed threatened species. The Swainson's hawk is an uncommon breeding resident in the Central Valley (Polite 2000). Swainson's hawks breeding in the Central Valley appear to winter in Mexico and Columbia (CDFG 2001). Bloom (1980) estimated 110 nesting pairs, and a total of 375 pairs in California (Polite 2000). The diet of the Swainson's hawk is varied, although its staple in the Central Valley is the California vole, augmented with a variety of bird and insect species. Over 85 percent of Swainson's hawk territories in the Central Valley are in riparian systems adjacent to suitable foraging habitats. Swainson's hawks often nest peripherally to riparian systems of the valley, as well as within lone trees or groves of trees in agricultural fields. Valley oak, Fremont cottonwood, walnut and large willow are the most commonly used nest trees in the Central Valley, each with an

Many species of concern have been seen on the Refuge including this tricolored blackbird.
Photo by USFWS

average mature height of about 58 feet, and ranging from 41 to 82 feet tall. Swainson's hawks require large, open grasslands with abundant prey in association with suitable nest trees. Suitable foraging areas include native grasslands or lightly grazed pastures, alfalfa and other hay crops and certain grain and row croplands. Unsuitable foraging habitat includes crops, such as vineyards, orchards, certain row crops, rice, corn and cotton crops. Suitable nest sites may be found in mature riparian forests, lone trees or groves of oaks, other trees in agricultural fields and mature roadside trees.

Declining numbers of Swainson's hawks are, in part, caused by loss of nesting habitat (Polite 2000). Converting compatible agricultural lands to residential and commercial developments and noncompatible agricultural activities are a serious threat to Swainson's hawks throughout California (CDFG 2000). Swainson's hawks have been seen on nearly the entire Refuge (B. Treiterer, USFWS, pers. comm.).

Other species that have been seen on the Refuge include the following State or Federal species of concern: white-faced ibis, tri-colored blackbird, western burrowing owl, oak titmouse (*Baeolophus inornatus*), white-tailed kite, loggerhead shrike, rufous hummingbird (*Selasphorus rufus*), lamprey (*Lampetra ayresii*), Pacific lamprey, small-footed bat (*Myotis ciliolabrum*) and Yuma myotis bat (*Myotis yumanensis*).

Visitor Services
Ecoregion Scale

Wildlife viewing is the most popular wildlife-dependent activity among ecoregion residents with 56 percent of outdoor recreationists participating. About 41 percent of residents participate in freshwater fishing, 19 percent in saltwater fishing and 9 percent in hunting.

The population in the ecoregion is expected to rise by 47 percent between the year 2000 and the year 2020. Unmet demand appears to be highest in the region for wildlife viewing, trail hiking, picnicking, camping and freshwater fishing with this trend expected to continue. Outdoor recreationists in the Central Valley/San Francisco Bay Ecoregion tend to be mostly white (78 percent) with growing participation by the Hispanic and Asian-American communities. In general, residents of moderate or high family incomes have the greatest interest in wildlife-dependent recreation, both consumptive and non-consumptive types.

The nearest other national wildlife refuges are Antioch Dunes, San Pablo Bay, Sutter and San Joaquin River. Of these, only Sutter

Wildlife viewing is the most popular wildlife-dependent activity among ecoregion residents with 56 percent of outdoor recreators participating.
Photo by USFWS

is open to unsupervised visitor use. Other nearby public lands offering similar wildlife-dependent recreational activities include the Yolo Basin Wildlife Area, Cosumnes River Preserve and the American River Parkway. The U.S. Forest Service and Bureau of Land Management have considerable land holdings in the ecoregion and all wildlife-dependent priority recreational uses are accommodated on various portions of their lands. There are 16 State Wildlife Areas or Ecological Areas operated by DFG within an hour's drive of the Refuge. These 16 areas provide opportunities for wildlife observation, interpretation, hunting and/or fishing. In addition, there are five State Parks within approximately one hour's drive that offer fishing, wildlife observation and/or interpretation.

Local Scale

More than 50 percent of lands within the Refuge's approved boundary are privately-owned and the Service has no authority to provide for visitor use of those lands. However, limited visitor use is available on Refuge lands that are owned by or over which the Service has management authority.

Wildlife-Dependent Recreation.
In the Refuge System Improvement Act of 1997, Congress recognized six wildlife-dependent priority recreational uses of refuges: hunting, fishing, wildlife observation and photography, interpretation and environmental education. More than 6,000 people per year visit the Refuge to participate in a variety of wildlife dependent recreational and educational activities. Currently, the Refuge accommodates waterfowl hunting, wildlife observation and photography, interpretation and environmental education.

Hunting. In 2004, the Service began a planning process for a public waterfowl hunt program on the South Stone Lake Unit of the Refuge. The first Refuge-managed hunt occurred during the 2005-2006 hunt season. The program consists of spaced-blinds accessible by foot and boat and emphasizes opportunities for youth and hunters in

wheelchairs. Prior to acquisition by the Service, waterfowl hunting had occurred on the South Stone Lake Unit on the Sun River and Lodi Gun Club properties while they were private duck hunting clubs. Some illegal waterfowl hunting also occurs occasionally in the Beach Lake, North Stone Lake, and South Stone Lake units due to limitations in Refuge law enforcement capability and opportunities to gain illegal access via private property and by boat.

Wildlife Observation and Photography. The Refuge, with its proximal location to a major urban center, wildlife diversity and mosaic of habitats, is steadily increasing in popularity with the surrounding community. The North Stone and Beach Lake units of the Refuge are open every second and fourth Saturday of each month (except during July and August) from 7:30 a.m. to 2:00 p.m. and 9:00 a.m. to 3:00 p.m., respectively. Visitors access the Refuge from the trailhead at the Elk Grove Boulevard entrance, west of Interstate-5. Refuge staff and/or volunteers greet visitors who may take a 3-mile round trip self-guided walk through grasslands on the North Stone Lake unit, past seasonal and permanent wetlands, and along riparian habitat to an observation platform overlooking Lower Beach Lake and wetland impoundments. Visitors in wheelchairs or with small children may drive directly to the universally accessible trail leading to the

The first Refuge-managed hunt occurred in the 2005/2006 hunt season, including this wheelchair accessible hunting blind on the Sun River Unit.
Photo by USFWS

viewing platform. Visitors typically spend between two and four hours per visit and there is no daily entrance fee.

Environmental Education. Since the establishment of the Refuge, educators and youth care professionals from Sacramento, San Joaquin and Yolo counties have been using the Refuge as an outdoor classroom to enhance course curricula. Educators include teachers, professors and outdoor education leaders. Youth care professionals include leaders for Scouts, 4H, Campfire and church groups. Most of the educators and youth care professionals who are served by the Refuge's environmental education program work with kindergarten through college age students. Currently, most educational field trips are guided by Refuge volunteers or staff on the Beach Lake Unit, with occasional classroom visits. These programs are available by special arrangement.

Interpretation. Current Refuge interpretation consists of interpretative panels on the wildlife viewing platform, Refuge brochures, special guided tours by Refuge volunteers and staff, Refuge website and special events

such as the Refuge's annual Walk on the Wildside event.

Fishing. The Refuge does not currently have a formal fishing program open to the public, although several points of illegal entry exist and are regularly used by shore and boat anglers.

Non-Priority Wildlife-Dependent Visitor Uses. Before its establishment as a national wildlife refuge, a number of visitor uses occurred on the Refuge. The EIS (USFWS 1992) described recreational resources and uses that were cited in "public comments on the draft EIS, staff of land management organizations and agencies in the study area, representatives of recreation and conservation groups, marina operators, Sacramento County Sheriff's Department boat patrol members and boaters who regularly recreate on the waterways in the study area." Many of these historic uses continue in addition a number of other authorized and unauthorized non-priority wildlife dependent visitor uses occur on the Refuge including: bird-watching and nature study (e.g., National Audubon Society annual "Christmas bird counts"); target

Refuge visitors may take a 3-mile round trip, self-guided walk through managed grasslands and along a riparian zone to an observation platform overlooking a managed wetland.
Photo by USFWS

shooting/firearm discharging; hunting (mostly pheasant and waterfowl); trapping (to control populations of burrowing animals, such as beaver, muskrat and mink to control levee damage); hiking and walking; water-oriented recreation such as motorized boating, canoeing, kayaking, waterskiing, house-boating, fishing and swimming/sunbathing; horseback riding; jogging; bicycling; ultralight flying; helicopter training; fruit and nut gathering; picnicking and camping; and natural history plant collecting.

Socioeconomic Demographics

The Refuge is located within Sacramento County, bounded by the city of Elk Grove on the east, and 15 miles south of downtown Sacramento. Sacramento County's population was estimated at over 1.36 million in 2005 (USCB 2006) and is projected to grow by almost 0.5 million by 2025 (SACOG 2000). Sacramento is by far the biggest city in the county; and even though the Greater Sacramento Region includes portions of five other counties, 65 percent of the city's population lives within Sacramento County. By percentage, Elk Grove was the fastest growing large U.S. city, between 2004 and 2005 (USDOC 2006). Elk Grove incorporated in 2000 with a population of 81,400 (SACOG 2000) and had reached 112,338 by July, 2005 (USDOC 2006).

In 2004, there were an estimated 649,782 citizens in the labor force in Sacramento County (ACS 2004). In 2005 unemployment averaged 4.8 percent and is projected to decline in 2006 to 4.6 percent (SFP 2006). The sectors of the economy accounting for the largest numbers of jobs in the county in 2004 were: management, professional and related occupations (35 percent); sales and office occupations (31 percent) and service occupations (15 percent) (ACS 2004). In 2004 Sacramento County per-capita income averaged $23,589 and median family income averaged $57,488 (ACS 2004). Of people over the age of 25, 16 percent did not have a high school diploma, 23 percent had a high school diploma or equivalency, 19 percent attained a bachelor's degree and 8 percent attained a graduate or professional degree

(ACS 2004). In 2004, approximately 10 percent of Sacramento County residents were living in poverty (ACS 2004).

The largest age group distributions in Sacramento county are: between 25 and 44 years old (30 percent); under 18 (28 percent) and between 45 and 64 (22 percent) (ACS 2004). The racial compositions of Sacramento County and the city of Elk Grove are relatively diverse. Sacramento County's population is composed of 54.4 percent Caucasians, 16.1 percent Hispanics, 12.9 percent Asians and 10.4 percent African Americans (ACS 2004). The most recent statistics available for Elk Grove, from 2000, show that Elk Grove has a slightly higher percentage of Asian people (17.6 percent) and slightly less African Americans, Hispanics and Caucasians when compared to Sacramento County in the aggregate (USCB 2000). In Sacramento County there was an estimated 181,077 households with one or more people under the age of 18, in 2004 (ACS 2004).

Despite increasing urbanization, agriculture continues to be an important economic sector in Sacramento County. Sacramento County ranked 27th, out of 58 counties, in the State for gross value of agricultural production for 2002-2003 (CASS 2004). The county's top ten farm commodities in 2002 were grapes, milk, nursery stock, pears, poultry, vegetable crops, rice, cattle, corn and livestock (CASS 2004). While agriculture continued to be an important sector of the economy, 0.92 percent of prime farmland and 5.05 percent of agricultural land was converted to urban and build-up uses between 1988 and 1998 (Kuminoff et al. 2000).

The median home price in Sacramento County jumped to $287,672 by 2004 (ACS 2004) and has continued to rise, reaching $360,000 by April of 2006 (CLMI 2006). Housing units in the county are projected to increase from 473,211 in 2000 to 662,004 in 2025 (SACOG 2000). Of the increase, 45 percent will occur in unincorporated areas, and 25 percent in the city of Sacramento, but fully 20 percent of the increase is projected to occur in Elk Grove where housing units increased from 24,817 in 2000 (SACOG 2000) to 66,733 in 2005 (CEG 2006).

Cultural Resources

Cultural Resources and Ethnographic Background

Cultural resources include a variety of links to past cultures, such as physical remains, sites, objects, records, oral histories and traditional culture, but can also include landscapes, plants, animals, sacred locations and traditional cultural properties that play a role in the traditional community. Other historic sites represent a wide variety of activities, including homesteading and settlement, trade, transportation, agriculture and ranching.

Most of the recorded cultural resources at the Refuge are archaeological sites linked with American Indian occupation that include large village sites, small seasonally occupied camps, sites with burials and sites considered sacred. The material remains of historic activities within the project boundary may include standing structures and foundations, still-occupied dwellings, abandoned trails, ferry sites, extant roadways and railroad lines.

The Plains Miwok formerly occupied the lands now within the approved Refuge boundary. The Refuge contains a rich array of Plains Miwok cultural history because its abundant flora and fauna made it a suitable place for humans. Before the area was settled by Euroamericans, the Plains Miwok territory extended from north of the lower reaches of the Cosumnes River to south of the lower reach of the Mokelumne River, along both sides of the Sacramento River and southwest to the vicinity of Mt Diablo in Contra Costa County. The eastern boundary of their territory was the foothills of the Sierra Nevada, which they shared with the Central Sierra Miwok (Levy 1978, Service 1992).

Typical of the surrounding Central California groups, the political organization of the Plains Miwok is believed to have centered around small tribelets. Each

tribelet was essentially sedentary and occupied a place more or less continuously for generations. Resources were variably controlled with acorn and hunting lands considered communal, while seed tracts and fishing stations could be individually allocated in accordance with inherited use rights for one or more seasons. The tribelets also used seasonal camps to exploit seasonal resources, such as salmon, acorns, etc. (Tremaine 1997, Kroeber 1932, Bennyhoff 1977).

Numerous Plains Miwok village locations were identified during the waning years of traditional American Indian inhabitation of the region. Major village sites are plotted along the Sacramento, Mokelumne and Cosumnes rivers. Additionally, several locations in Sacramento County have been identified as sacred by the Native American Heritage Commission. The "Hulpoomne" appears to be the nearest known "tribe" associated with the north portion of the Refuge, being associated with a principal village in the area where the town of Freeport now stands (Merriam 1907).

Today, descendants of the Plains Miwok continue to have ties to their ancestral lands. Known cultural sites on and off Refuge lands have been identified and efforts have been made to work with tribal representatives to restore native habitats while preserving these sites. In some cases and at the request of tribal representatives, previously-disturbed archeological sites have been capped with layers of soil and vegetation to help prevent human remains and other objects from being exposed on the surface. The comprehensive conservation planning process gives us the opportunity to plan for the future of the Refuge, working to protect these important resources and providing a link to the past for current generations of Plains Miwok.

Historic Setting

Spanish explorers arriving in the 1700s were the first people other than American Indians to enter the Sacramento Valley area. For the most part, the region was little affected by Spanish occupation, being removed from the missions' sphere of influence. Land in the Sacramento Valley was not claimed for private ownership until Mexican land grants were issued in the 1830s. The Rio Ojotska land grant, issued in 1833 to J.B.R. Cooper, was the earliest land grant given in the area; however, the recipient failed to lay claim to the land and renounced the grant the following year (USFWS 1992).

New Helvetia, established by John A. Sutter in 1839 near the present site of Sacramento, was the first Euroamerican settlement in the valley. Sutter obtained 11 leagues of land through a grant from the Mexican government, which approved of Sutter's plan to build a fort and establish order on the edges of their frontier. Sutter's Fort was founded with goods purchased from the Russians when Fort Ross was abandoned in 1841. A large number of horses and cattle were brought to Sutter's Fort, along with a cannon and several pieces of artillery. These accoutrements gave the fort a military appearance, which undoubtedly discouraged skirmishes between the settlers and American Indians (USFWS 1992).

Lands along the Cosumnes River, northeast of the Refuge, were claimed in 1844 by two employees of Sutter. At the time, the Cosumnes area was "thickly populated by Indians" (USFWS 1992). The land, which was claimed to graze cattle, was called Rancho Omochumnes after the local American Indian tribelet. Another land grant, Sanjon de los Moquelumnes, included the southeastern portion of the Refuge; this land grant was also named after a Plains Miwok tribelet.

In 1848, California and the Sacramento Valley were changed forever by the discovery of gold in the Sierra Nevada foothills. Until that time, most of California had been unaffected by Euroamerican settlement. With the discovery of gold, thousands of miners entered the state. Thousands of settlers soon followed the miners. Sacramento was the main community, surrounded by dozens of smaller settlements. In the beginning, the locations of early towns coincided with mining activities. Probably only limited mining occurred in the vicinity of the Refuge because of the scarcity of gold-bearing gravels at such low elevations. Later, as agricultural pursuits replaced mining, farming communities appeared. By the 1860s, agricultural enterprises were well established in the Sacramento Valley and the Delta region. A variety of crops were grown on and west of the Refuge while areas to the east were used for mixed agriculture and to raise livestock. Towns that were established near the Refuge include Franklin, Bruceville, Locke, Sheldon and Wilton.

Archeology

Requests have been submitted to the North Central Information Center of the California Archaeological Inventory for information regarding the types and location of archeological sites on and in the vicinity of the Refuge. Historic and ethnographic sources were also reviewed for information pertaining to the area.

Types of Archeological Sites. Intensive prehistoric and historic habitation and use in the Sacramento area has resulted in a large and diverse archeological resource base. Over 450 archeological sites have been recorded in Sacramento County. Many sites have been recorded, although most lands within the approved Refuge boundary have not been surveyed systematically for cultural resources.

Most of the recorded sites within the vicinity of the Refuge are prehistoric in nature. Although this is partly because prehistoric site density is greater than historic site density in the Refuge area, it is also because most archeologists working in the area did not record historic sites until quite recently. Sites associated with American Indian occupation include large sites, small, seasonally occupied camps, sites with burials and sites that were considered sacred. Historic sites represent a wide variety of activities, including homesteading and settlement, trade, transportation, agriculture and ranching. The material remains of these activities probably include standing structures and foundation, still occupied dwellings, abandoned trails and ferry sites, extant roadways and railroad lines.

Location of Archeological Sites. Both prehistoric and historic sites within and around the Refuge tend to be located on high ground near permanent water sources. Determining areas of historic sensitivity is difficult, however, because of the lack of identified historic period sites within the Refuge. For the most part, early historic settlements (before the establishment of reliable flood control measures) were located on prehistoric sites. In fact, it is common to find a prehistoric midden site under a historic dwelling because American Indians often chose to live on topographic high points. American Indian habitation sites became even higher points of land as their refuse accumulated over hundreds or even thousands of years of occupation, and these mounds were attractive building locations for early settlers. In addition to topographic high points, historic remains should be expected near early settlement locations, along railroad lines and near ferry sites.

Many prehistoric archeological sites have been identified along major drainages, such as the Mokelumne and Cosumnes rivers and Laguna, Skunk, Badger and Deer creeks. Many unidentified sites are probably present on these drainages although intensive, systematic surveys have never been done. Additional areas of prehistoric sensitivity include the lands around Beach, North, and South Stone lakes and Snodgrass and Bear sloughs.

Land Use
Natural biologic communities presently occurring within the entire approved Refuge project boundary encompass a total of 8,283 acres and include: annual grasslands (71 percent), seasonal wetlands (13 percent), perennial wetlands (7 percent), riparian forest and scrub shrub (5 percent), deepwater aquatic habitat (3 percent) and oak woodlands (1 percent). Existing agricultural cover types within the Refuge occupy an additional 10,321 acres and are comprised of: corn (28 percent), pasture (21 percent), range (17 percent), wheat (8 percent), sugar beets (8 percent), grapes (7 percent), other field crops (4 percent), pears (2 percent) and tomatoes (1 percent).

Adjacent lands in this region are shifting from low density, rural, residential homes and structures, agriculture, and recreational areas to medium density single family suburban tract homes, master-planned communities and vineyards (B. Treiterer, USFWS, pers. comm.).

Wilderness and Other Special Management Areas
As required by Service planning policy, a wilderness review (Appendix G) was conducted for the Refuge. None of the Refuge lands were eligible for wilderness designation.

Current Management Practices
The primary management focus of the Refuge is enhancing, restoring and maintaining wetlands, riparian woodlands, grasslands and valuable agricultural lands. Wetland habitats include permanent and seasonal wetlands, including vernal pools, riparian woodlands, open water and aquatic beds.

Wetlands
Water Management. As an integral part of the Refuge program, the Service manages water on seasonal and permanent wetlands on the South Stone Lake, Headquarters and Beach Lake units totaling approximately 335 acres. Sources of water for managed Refuge wetland units include SP Cut, Lower Beach Lake, Sacramento Drainage Canal and South Stone Lake. A total of seven surface pumping stations draw water from Refuge waterways to manage wetland impoundments on the Refuge. Water control structures (i.e., screw gates) are also used to manage water entering other permanent wetlands areas, such as North Stone Lake and Parker Slough and portions of the Sun River property. The overall water flow in the SP Cut is controlled by screw and flap gates passing under Lambert Bridge, upstream drainage, groundwater levels and irrigation return flows.

Flood up, drawdown and summer irrigations are planned to provide habitat for migrating, wintering and breeding water birds. Timing of flood up is constrained to varying degrees by the amount of water available under appropriative and riparian water rights in any given year and to minimize mosquito production.

Permanent Wetlands. Permanent wetlands are managed to provide brood rearing habitat during the summer months for waterfowl and other waterbirds and year round habitat for other species, including bitterns, herons and marsh wrens. Periodic draw downs of the permanent wetlands on the Beach Lake, Headquarters and South Stone Lake units are done when vegetation, such as cattails and tules, covers more than 75 percent of the surface area and to control undesirable fish species such as carp. These treatments occur approximately every three to five years. Not more than three out of the five permanent wetland impoundments on these units are drawn down in any given year, in order to maintain habitat for the federally-threatened giant garter snake and summer resident birds. In other permanent wetlands, such as Parker Slough, North Stone Lake, and the Sun River property, water levels can be manipulated using screw gates to lower levels, but not completely de-water wetlands. In these situations, the goals are to stimulate growth of desirable moist soil plants along pond edges and allow for some control of dense vegetation, if necessary.

Seasonal Wetlands. Seasonal wetlands are managed to provide feeding and loafing habitat for the thousands of migratory waterbirds that winter in the Central Valley and make use of the Beach-Stone Lakes Basin. During years with no restrictions on water use, flood ups begin in early to mid-September and continue through mid-October. To minimize mosquito production, impoundments are rapidly filled to a maximum depth of one to two feet. Occasional pumping may be required during the winter if rainfall levels are below normal. Drawdowns commence in early April and continue through mid-June.

Varying the draw down schedule in wetland units stimulates production of different plants. Early draw downs favor grasses, such as swamp timothy and watergrass; late drawdowns favor smartweeds and some undesirable plants, such as cocklebur. Late drawdowns occur in one or two wetland units per year to provide habitat for nesting shorebirds, including black-necked stilts (*Himantopus mexicanus*), American avocets (*Recurvirostra Americana*) and Wilson's phalaropes (*Phalaropus tricolor*). Summer irrigations are designed to stimulate the growth of high quality foods for waterfowl, such as swamp timothy and watergrass. These are done in late July and early August when the unit is flooded to a depth of 12 inches and then drawn down. Close coordination with the Sacramento/Yolo Mosquito Vector Control District is essential to minimize mosquito production on managed wetlands.

SP Cut. Water levels in the SP Cut are controlled by screw and flap gates passing under Lambert Bridge, upstream drainage, groundwater levels and irrigation return flows. Through informal agreement with Sacramento County Department of Water Resources, the screw gate on the Lambert Bridge flood control structure is operated by a local landowner to manage availability of upstream water for irrigation and wetland management. Water levels are generally higher during the summer months when the gate at Lambert Bridge is open and farmers upstream are irrigating crops. During the winter, water levels are determined by rainfall levels and drainage entering from upstream. During large rainfall events, water enters SP Cut when floodwaters overtop the Morrison Creek dam at the north end of Lower Beach Lake.

North Stone Lake. North Stone Lake is roughly 260 acres in size with depths ranging from 0.5 feet to 8.0 feet. Water enters the lake via concrete culverts under Interstate-5 that bring water from upstream developed areas to the east and from SP Cut to the west, through a single pipe fitted with a screw gate. Water levels in the lake can be manipulated to a limited degree (12 inches maximum) by opening or closing this screw gate, depending on water fluctuations in the SP Cut. There are no control structures on the Interstate-5 culverts.

South Stone Lake. Water levels in various parts of South Stone Lake fluctuate with levels in SP Cut and tidal influences from downstream of Lambert Bridge. As with North Stone Lake, water levels are highest during the summer irrigation months and winter rainfall months. Except for requesting opening of the screw gate at Lambert Bridge, Refuge staff have little control over water levels in South Stone Lake.

Habitat Manipulations. Managed wetlands are dynamic systems that require periodic habitat manipulations to maintain a desired successional stage, optimal for feeding, loafing, breeding waterfowl and waterbirds. Mowing, prescribed burning, discing and noxious weed control during late summer are all part of efforts to manage less desirable vegetation with limited food value for migratory waterbirds, such as cocklebur and spike rushes. These activities also improve conditions for grasses and forbs to grow, such as watergrass, swamp timothy, smartweeds as well as other desirable vegetation, such as bulrush, buttonbush and willow. Each unit is evaluated annually to determine the need for manipulations. Permanent wetland units are disced every three to five years to maintain an equal ratio of open water to vegetation. Seasonal wetlands are disced or mowed every other year, depending on vegetation response. The perimeter of each wetland is disced to enhance access by mosquito fish and water management.

Mosquito Control

The Refuge staff works closely with the Sacramento/Yolo Mosquito Vector Control District (SYMVCD) to reduce or eliminate production of mosquitos on the Refuge. In accordance with the EIS (USFWS 1992), the Refuge entered into an MOU with SYMVCD in 1993. This MOU outlines an effective mosquito suppression program that includes biological and chemical

controls to be used on the Refuge, wetland design and water level and vegetation management recommendations and research partnerships. Biological controls include the placement of mosquito fish and guppies (*Poecilia reticulate*) in permanent and seasonal wetlands and the use of *Bacillus thuringiensis israeliensis* (Bti) and *B. sphaericus*, which are effective at controlling certain life stages of mosquito larvae with minimal non-target organism impacts. Any pesticides to be used on the Refuge must be approved by the Service prior to the onset of mosquito season in early spring. Pesticides may target mosquito larvae and adults and may include aerial applications, as well as ultra-low volume ground application. In keeping with the MOU, the Refuge consults with SYMVCD to ensure wetlands are designed to minimize mosquito habitat. For example, berms along some managed wetland units are graded with a slope of 1.5-2.0 feet horizontal to 1.0 foot vertical to limit the growth of marginal vegetation. Furthermore, the perimeters of seasonal wetlands may be disced to enhance access by foraging mosquito fish to larvae. Wetlands are also designed and constructed to allow for rapid flooding and draw down.

Riparian

Agricultural conversion, water conveyance, and flood control, and other changes in land use have eliminated much of the original riparian and oak woodland habitat from the Beach-Stone Lakes Basin. Overall, the Central Valley has lost over 95 percent of its wooded riparian habitats. Within the approved Refuge boundary, the widths of riparian forest corridors vary from 10-300 feet wide along Morrison Creek, SP Cut, Parker Slough, the south arm and smaller branches of North Stone Lake, and South Stone Lake (see Figure 5, Vegetation Map). The only mature valley oak forest remaining in the basin exists along Morrison Creek. Restoration efforts on the Beach Lake, North Stone Lake, Headquarters and South Stone Lake units have expanded riparian zones by 100-120 acres.

Restoration practices include planting a variety of riparian trees, such as Fremont cottonwood, willow, box elder, sycamore,, valley oak and associated understory shrubs and grasses and then providing supplemental irrigation and weeding for a period of three to five years to facilitate plant establishment. In the case of valley oaks, both planting acorns with no watering and seedlings with watering have been used with success. Choosing an appropriate site based on soil type and elevation is the most important aspect of a successful restoration project.

Grasslands

Grasslands once covered vast stretches of the Central Valley, supporting extirpated species, such as pronghorn antelope, tule elk (*Cervus elaphus nannodes*), grizzly bear and millions of waterfowl and other migratory birds. These grasslands supported seasonal wetlands such as vernal pools and wet meadows populated by perennial and annual grasses. Over 98 percent of Central Valley native grasslands have been converted to agriculture and urban development or displaced by exotic vegetation. . Many native annual grassland species no longer occur and have been replaced by nonnative annuals such as annual rye. The remaining grasslands are now a mix of native and nonnative species.

The North Stone Lake Unit of the Refuge supports one of the only remaining continuous tracts of un-leveled grasslands in the eastern Sacramento-San Joaquin Delta region, with approximately 1,900 acres of annual and perennial grasslands. Preservation of this remnant grassland topography is a high priority. Other small (one to 21 acres) areas exist on the Beach Lake and Headquarters units. General management goals for the North Stone Lake Unit are to: maintain and expand existing native grasses, such as creeping wild rye (*Leymus triticoides*), meadow barley (*Hordeum brachyantherum*), and sedges; minimize the fire hazard posed by accumulated dead grasses; control the spread of noxious weeds; and provide habitats for grassland-dependent species, including greater sandhill cranes, arctic nesting geese, white-faced ibises, long-billed curlews, western meadowlarks, horned

larks, and birds of prey, including Swainson's hawks, burrowing owls, and northern harriers. These management goals are being accomplished through implementation of a cattle grazing program, small-scale prescribed burning, and aggressive noxious weed control.

The Refuge grazing program on the North Stone Lake Unit consists of running cattle on the dry pasture from November through mid-June, until annual grasses turn brown. Some cattle are then moved to the 172 acres of irrigated pasture on the unit from June through October. Cattle stocking rates vary in the five dry pastures depending on rainfall, timing, quantity and frequency, with a target of 1,500-2,000 pounds of Residual Dry Matter (RDM) in three of the five pastures and 2,000-4,000 pounds of RDM in the remaining two pastures. The irrigated pastures are stocked at a rate of one animal unit month (AUM), which is the amount of forage needed by a cow and her suckling calf for one month, per one to two acres. Following a 10-year period during which grazing had been curtailed on the North Stone Lake Unit, use by sandhill cranes, long-billed curlews, white-fronted geese, and other waterfowl has increased substantially on the unit after the Refuge re-introduced a grazing program in 1999. Excluding cattle from the majority of riparian areas through fencing was completed in 2003. Other measures to improve management of the unit will include developing alternative watering sources ,erosion control measures near the irrigated pastures, noxious weed control and continued monitoring of wildlife responses.

The Refuge holds title to a conservation easement on the 1,400-acre Wetland Preserve Unit that supports a mixture of natural and man made vernal pools and

General restoration goals for the grasslands on the North Stone Lake Unit are to: maintain and expand existing native grasses, decrease the fire danger, control noxious weeds and provide habitat for a variety of grassland dependent species like this Swainson's hawk.
Photo by USFWS

seasonal wetlands. Recent studies at the Cosumnes River Preserve (J. Marty, TNC, pers. comm.) indicate that a managed grazing program is most effective at maintaining and enhancing vernal pool plant and animal species. Grazing conducted by the landowner from November through June on the preserve results in a RDM rate of 600 to 800 pounds and is ideal to reduce competition between vernal pool plants and nonnative grasses, such as annual rye grass, and noxious weeds, such as yellow starthistle (*Centaurea solstitialis*). Refuge staff are working with representatives of the landowner, AKT Development Corporation, to develop a grazing program that will protect and enhance seasonal wetlands on the preserve.

Weed Control

Since 1995, the Refuge has adopted an active aquatic and terrestrial weed management program in the Beach-Stone Lakes Basin, particularly as a founding member of the Stone Lakes Water Hyacinth Control Group. The Refuge conducts treatments for control of water hyacinth under a Statewide National Pollution Discharge Elimination System (NPDES) General Permit (No. CAG990005) for discharge of aquatic pesticides. The Refuge and SRCSD utilize Reward (Diquat) and Aquamaster (glyphosphate) to control water hyacinth in the basin. Another aquatic species, Brazilian elodea (*Egeria densa*), is also abundant in waterways and may emerge as a management concern as opportunities for recreational boating are developed on the Refuge.

The Refuge Integrated Pest Management approach used to control weeds relies on burning, mowing, grazing, discing and herbicide applications. Due to the persistence and abundance of most weeds in the environment and regulatory constraints on use of fire, chemical applications are the only currently effective method for controlling water hyacinth, perennial pepperweed (*Lepidium latifolium*) and yellow star thistle. The Refuge uses Transline and Telar to control yellow star thistle and perennial

pepperweed, respectively. Mechanical control methods tend to spread, rather than control, perennial pepperweed. Potential biological control organisms, including water hyacinth-eating weevils (*Neochitina* spp.) and moths (*Sameodes albiguttlilis*), have been introduced into the Delta through a cooperative program with the U.S. Department of Agriculture, Agricultural Research Service (USDA-ARS) and California Department of Food and Agriculture (CDFA) to evaluate control of water hyacinth. Unfortunately, these biological control agents have not been affective in reducing stands of water hyacinth. Given the vast amounts of hyacinth produced each year on the Refuge and its inaccessibility to equipment, mechanical control is not feasible. Mechanical removal in isolated water ways would be prohibitively expensive, costing an estimated $80,000 annually and accessing sites with heavy equipment would likely cause significant impacts to sensitive habitats. Non-chemical methods to prevent the spread of water hyacinth include deploying log booms at strategic locations to prevent spread, screening culverts to prevent re-introduction and removing water hyacinth from small water bodies by hand. The Refuge also participates in the Sacramento Weed Abatement Team which is coordinated by the Sacramento County Agricultural Commission.

Farming Program

A variety of migratory birds, including waterfowl, long-billed curlew, black-bellied plover, white-faced ibis and sandhill cranes, feed on waste grain and invertebrates remaining in agricultural fields after harvest. These migratory birds depend on farm fields of small grains, alfalfa, tomatoes, etc. for a marked portion of their diet. Therefore, it is vital that the Service, private landowners, and Sacramento County cooperate to maintain viable "wildlife friendly" agriculture in the vicinity of the Refuge. Except for the grazing programs that the Refuge oversees, cooperative farming on Refuge lands currently is limited to the Headquarters Unit. To date, the goal of the farming program has been to maintain the fields in corn, wheat, safflower, or grass to provide habitat for wildlife and control weeds until a larger scale restoration project is implemented.

Monitoring and Surveys

A variety of surveys and studies have been conducted by Service staff, volunteers and students on the Refuge since its establishment. These studies are primarily intended to evaluate the effectiveness of management activities and monitor the status of biological resources. A summary of ongoing surveys and studies and their objectives follows.

- Colonial waterbird survey. Rookeries of nesting great blue heron, great egrets, and double-crested cormorants are monitored yearly to determine abundance, distribution and nesting success.
- Landbird monitoring program. A cooperative mist netting and bird banding program is conducted in selected areas with SYMVCD to monitor and document bird diversity and relative abundance. The program is also investigating the role of wild bird populations as reservoirs for mosquito-borne diseases such as Western equine encephalitis virus, St. Louis encephalitis virus and west Nile virus.
- Modesto song sparrow study. As part of the landbird banding program, song sparrows are also color banded on the South Stone Lake Unit in an ongoing effort to determine nesting success and survival of young.
- Weekly waterfowl survey, October through May. Waterbird (waterfowl, shorebirds and cranes) counts are done weekly during the fall, winter and spring to determine population trends and use patterns.
- Plant surveys. Vegetation in moist soil wetlands is qualitatively surveyed each spring to guide management actions such as discing, mowing and timing of summer irrigations.
- Noxious weed surveys. Refuge units are surveyed and mapped with GPS equipment to monitor noxious weeds such as yellow starthistle, perennial pepperweed and water hyacinth.
- Pasture monitoring A residual dry matter survey (measure of the amount of dry

A cooperative mist netting and bird banding program is conducted in selected areas with the Sacramento-Yolo Mosquito and Vector Control District to monitor and document the diversity and relative abundance of bird species, such as this blue grosbeak, and to evaluate their role in the transmission of mosquito-borne viruses.
Photo by USFWS

grass remaining after the growing season) is conducted annually to adjust grazing rates for the upcoming year.

The following studies have been completed primarily by graduate students on the Refuge:

- Western pond turtle survey. Determined turtle survival and reproductive success.
- Native grass. Determined effects of various treatments (e.g., burning, grazing and no treatment) on three species of native grasses on the North Stone Lake Unit.
- Nitrogen. Determined the role increased nitrogen levels may play in exotic weed expansions along freeway corridors.
- Sunflower moth. Evaluating the relationship between the California sunflower and its parasitoids.
- Bats. Conducted presence or absence surveys on selected sites on the Refuge.
- Aquatic surveys. Conducted fish, amphibian, and reptile surveys to determine presence and absence of various species.

Further refinement of survey and monitoring protocol for the Refuge is needed. Additional baseline inventories need to be completed and a relational database should be developed to store and access monitoring and inventory data.

4 Challenges

Invasive Species

As defined in Executive Order 13112, an invasive species is an alien species whose introduction does or is likely to cause economic or environmental harm or harm to human health. Invasive species can impact human health, interfere with agriculture and aquaculture, interfere with water delivery, increase flooding and erosion, block access to water ways, decrease habitat for native plants and animals and compete with native species for resources. Invasive species are one of the most critical nationwide challenges facing national wildlife refuges (NWRA 2002). The Service and other bureaus within the Department of the Interior have been working to eradicate invasive species on Federal lands and are partnering with State agencies and local organizations to restore ecosystems with native plants and species. By 1998, the battle against invasive species was costing the Refuge System an estimated $13 million per year (NWRA 2002). By 2002 a $150 million backlog of critical invasive species projects had been identified within the Refuge System (NWRA 2002). Most current management practices are aimed at control and eradication of existing invasive species; much work remains to prevent introduction of additional invasive species, educate the public and to fund more research and monitoring.

A large number of invasive species now reside on the Refuge. Vertebrate invasive species found on the Refuge that are well established in the region include European starlings (*Sturnus vulgaris*), rock doves (*Columba livia*), American bullfrogs red-eared sliders, feral dogs (*Canis lupus familiaris*), feral cats (*Felis silvestris*), black rats (*Rattus rattus*), Norway rats (*Rattus norvegicus*) and house mice

(*Mus musculus*). The majority of fishes occurring in Sacramento-San Joaquin Delta and Refuge waterbodies are non-native , including carp, catfish, sunfish and largemouth bass. Except for capture of feral dogs and cats and localized reductions of rodents near buildings and carp from wetland impoundments, no active control of these species is currently conducted or planned. As urban areas expand, we expect to see increases in feral dogs and cats, rock doves and great basin Canada geese. Preliminary studies at the Cosumnes River Preserve indicate black rats are negatively affecting reproductive success in a variety of songbirds nesting in mature valley oak riparian forest. Invasive invertebrates found on the Refuge, such as various species of mosquitos and mitten crab (*Eriocheir sinensis*), may act as hosts to various diseases. Control of mosquito populations is addressed in Chapter 3 under Current Management. Mosquitos are a vector for western equine encephalomyelitis virus. St Louis encephalitis and west Nile virus that can cause disease in humans. Mitten crabs can act as a host to the Asian lung fluke (*Paragonimus westermani*), which can cause disease in humans and other mammals if consumed without thorough cooking (ANSTF 2003).

Methods used to control invasive weeds include chemical, mechanical (including mowing, discing and hand removal) and biological control. The majority of grasslands on the Refuge and throughout California are now composed of nonnative annual grasses, such as annual rye, soft chess (*Bromus hordeaceus*), wild oats and Mediterranean barley (*Hordeum marinum*). Himalayan blackberries (*Rubus armeniacus*) are prevalent in riparian zones and along waterways. Invasive tree species on the Refuge include black locust (*Robinia pseudoacacia*) and osage orange (*Maclura pomifera*). Many of these invasive species have replaced native vegetation, but are so well established that eradication would be nearly impossible. Current control and eradication efforts concentrate on three noxious weeds that require immediate attention (Table 1). Other species being considered for monitoring, control and eradication from grassland, aquatic, and riparian habitats include: medusahead grass (*Taeniatherum caput-medusae*), barbed goat grass (*Aegilops triuncialis*), Brazilian elodea, and giant reed (*Arundo donax*).

Basin Hydrology and Water Quality
Floodplain Conditions

The hydrologic regime and configuration of the 100-year floodplain in the Beach-Stone Lakes Basin have been dramatically altered when compared with historic pre-settlement conditions. Changes to the landscape have included: (1) completion of the Sacramento River levee system and Sacramento Flood Control Project; (2) dam placement on the Mokelumne River; (3) construction of the Southern Pacific Railroad; (4) reclamation of tracts and islands in the basin for farming;

and (5) constricting of downstream channel capacities due to raising of levees.

The approved Refuge boundary lies entirely within the 100-year floodplain of Morrison Creek and the Cosumnes and Mokelumne rivers and the current 100-year flood elevation is 16.00 feet above mean sea level. Damaging floods have occurred in the Beach-Stone Lakes basin an average of one out of every three years (USACE 1987, Hart 1999). Extensive flooding occurred in 14 of the last 40 years. The primary source of water during flood events is from the accumulated flows of the 192 square mile watershed of the Morrison Creek Stream Group (Morrison, Elder, Unionhouse, Florin and Laguna creeks). During high water events, Morrison Creek drains from east to west, then south through Beach Lake, North Stone Lake, and South Stone and finally through the Lambert Road bridge to Snodgrass Slough, thence into the North Mokelumne River. Alternately or concurrently, flood waters may flow south to north from the Cosumnes and Mokelumne Rivers up Snodgrass Slough and the Sacramento Drainage Canal, over the top of the Lambert Road bridge and into SP Cut

Table 1. Invasive Plant Species Targeted for Control on Stone Lakes National Wildlife Refuge.

Common Name	Scientific Name	**State Noxious Listing	Distribution and Origin
perennial pepperweed	*Lepidium latifolium*	B	waterways, riparian restoration sites, grasslands and along roadsides
yellow starthistle	*Centaurea solstitialis*	C	grasslands, roadsides
water hyacinth	*Eichhornia crassipes*	none	waterways, permanent wetlands, lakes
Brazilian elodea	*Egeria densa*	none	waterways, permanent wetlands, lakes
giant reed	*Arundo donax*	none	waterways, ditches
black locust	*Robinia pseudoacacia*	none	ornamental landscapes
osage orange	*Maclura pomifera*	none	hedgerows, ornamental landscapes
medusa head grass	*Taeniatherum caput-medusae*	C	grasslands

**"B"—Eradication, containment, control or other holding action at the discretion of the commissioner. "C"—State endorsed holding action and eradication only when found in a nursery; action to retard spread outside of nurseries at the discretion of the commissioner; reject only when found in a cropseed for planting or at the discretion of the commissioner (CDFA 2006).

and the Beach-Stone Lakes basin. Cosumnes and Mokelumne river flows may also enter the basin from the west by backing up along and passing under the Western Pacific Railroad grade. The flood season normally extends from November through April (USFWS 1992).

The Refuge receives storm water runoff from upstream urban developments, including Laguna West, Lakeside and Stonelake, which flow into Beach Lake and North Stone Lake. Projections are that continued urbanization will lead to a loss of upstream storage area and a doubling of storm water runoff entering the Stone Lakes basin. Build-out of the East Franklin, Poppy Ridge, Laguna Ridge and Lent Ranch projects east of Franklin Boulevard, will result in an additional 10,000 acres of urban development between Interstate-5 and Highway 99. This may lead to increases in both the elevation of the 100-year floodplain and duration of downstream flooding (CEG 2000). Under this scenario, impacts are anticipated to Refuge infrastructure, habitats and wildlife.

Increases in elevation and duration of flooding resulting from upstream development may affect the grassland, riparian and wetland habitats and associated wildlife now using the Refuge. Noxious weeds, such as perennial pepperweed, yellow star thistle and other species, may become more invasive on grassland habitats as seed sources are washed into the Refuge. Long term monitoring will be necessary to document changes in the nature of grasslands. Riparian habitats may be affected due to prolonged high flood water levels, particularly during the spring. Conversion of stands of willows and cottonwood trees in low lying areas to more aquatic habitats may result and the composition of seasonal and permanent wetlands may change.

Migratory birds that frequent large expanses of open water may benefit from these habitat conversions, such as white pelicans and tundra swans and the composition of local duck populations may shift from dabbling ducks, such as mallard and northern pintails, to diving ducks, such as canvasbacks (*Aythya valisineria*) and lesser scaup (*Aythya affinis*). Reduction in the availability of high ground for high water refugia may further impact listed species such as the giant garter snake and valley elderberry longhorn beetle.

More frequent and longer flooding events could also affect management of the grazing program on the North Stone Lake Unit of the Refuge. From November through mid July, cattle are rotated among five pasture units and during heavy rainfall events, they are moved from the southern to the northern pastures in anticipation of

Some species that frequent large expanses of open water, such as white pelicans, may benefit from more frequent flooding of the Refuge.
Photo by USFWS

flooding. Floodwaters rose 6 inches an hour during heavy rains in the winter of 2000, making unsafe conditions for driving the cattle north. Similar heavy rains during the winter of 2005/2006 also required relocation of cattle grazing. Increases in storm water flows could exacerbate this situation which may result in shortening of the grazing period.

Flood Control Projects

In addition to ongoing upstream development, hydrologic regimes on the Refuge may also be affected by new projects that could alter the configuration or depth of the 100-year floodplain. The hydrology of the Mokelumne and Cosumnes rivers and the Morrison Creek watershed has been studied extensively for various potential flood control projects by the USACE, California Department of Water Resources, City of Sacramento and Sacramento County. These projects include a recently completed project by Sacramento Area Flood Control Agency and the USACE to raise and re-configure levees along Morrison Creek and a project by Teichert to realign Laguna Creek for gravel extraction, which may decrease summertime flows from reaching Beach Lake.

Since the mid-1980s, Sacramento County has been exploring the feasibility of implementing a flood control project in the basin that could reduce the extent of the 100-year floodplain and in particular, decrease flooding in the community of Point Pleasant in southern Sacramento County. In 1998, the County Board of Supervisors adopted the Beach-Stone Lakes Flood Control Plan, outlining county policies for reducing flooding in the basin. Most recently, the County has convened a facilitated private and public stakeholder forum to explore alternatives for reducing or compensating for flood damages to landowners in the Beach-Stone Lakes basin. The forum will report back to the County Board of Supervisors with the results of their deliberations regarding a potential regional project to attenuate peak flood flows or improve flood conveyance. The County will then utilize engineering studies and the forum results to prepare a report on key findings of this effort.

Water Quality
Water quality is an important component in determining the overall function of the Refuge area ecosystem and is a major factor in determining the health of wildlife, aquatic organisms and fisheries. Water, sediment, and biota samples collected from eight locations indicate that levels of heavy metals, although present, were not sufficient to cause deleterious impacts to wildlife; however, concentrations of selenium in all five waterbodies tested are above levels recommended for the protection of aquatic life (USFWS 1992).

The Refuge is virtually surrounded by urban and agricultural areas. Environmental contaminants on the Refuge or in the area have the potential to accumulate on the Refuge and affect large numbers of fish and wildlife. Agricultural lands to the east, south, and southwest are potential sources of contaminants to Snodgrass Slough, as well as to South and North Stone lakes. Many small waterways and seasonal swales connect the agricultural lands with the Snodgrass Slough and North and South Stone lakes. The City of Sacramento is another potential contaminant source. Morrison Creek runs through southern Sacramento prior to entering the north end of the Refuge and has been characterized by the Environmental Protection Agency (EPA) as an impaired waterway because of high Diazinon concentrations. The EPA found that Diazinon poses unacceptable risks to agricultural workers and to birds and other wildlife species. Diazinon can overstimulate the nervous system, causing nausea, dizziness and confusion and at very high exposures caused by accidents or major spills, it can also cause death.

Additional studies of water quality conducted by Service Contaminants staff from 1999 to 2000 found that levels of pesticides with Diazinon in Morrison Creek were sufficient to cause mortality in bioassay organisms after rainfall greater than one inch. Most likely these pesticides were flushed through the stormwater runoff drainage system after accumulating on lawns and other areas during the dry season. Also see Chapter 3, Contaminants and Water Quality.

Sacramento County's National Pollutant Discharge Elimination System (NPDES) Municipal Permit requires reduction of pollutants found in urban stormwater runoff to the maximum extent possible. Stormwater detention basins are constructed as urban expanses east and upstream of the Refuge are developed. These basins are effective in reducing pollutants by 30 percent to 90 percent. The pollutants that are not detained will likely enter the Refuge in runoff, potentially affecting fish and wildlife.

Land Use Changes
Urbanization and Vineyard Conversion

Elk Grove incorporated as a city in 2000 and had the fastest growth rate for any large U.S. city between July 2004 and July 2005 (USDOC 2006). The city adopted its general plan in November 2003. When the City of Elk Grove incorporated, it adopted as a feature of its general plan, the urban service boundary previously identified in the Sacramento County General Plan, which defines the limit of urban development in the County. A 90-acre portion of the Wetland Preserve Unit of the Refuge lies within Elk Grove's city limit. As provided for in the Elk Grove general plan, approximately 8,000 acres of former agricultural land east and upstream of the Refuge is now being developed into residences, a regional shopping mall and office parks. Over 18,000 additional homes are expected to be constructed by 2010 on land previously supporting dry and irrigated pastureland and crops (SACOG 2000). Many migratory birds which frequent the Refuge are also dependent on habitats outside of the Refuge. For example, the greater sandhill crane has a wintering range of approximately three square miles (G. Ivey, pers. comm. 2003). Therefore, cranes utilizing the Refuge also rely on nearby agricultural fields, grasslands and wetlands for feeding, loafing, etc. As open land is lost, these birds are either forced to fly longer distances to suitable habitat or pushed into smaller and smaller parcels. Over the last ten years, the ability of the eastern Sacramento-San Joaquin Delta region to support wintering cranes and other species such as long-billed curlew, white-faced ibis, burrowing owl and Swainson's hawk has declined and continues to be threatened by urban development and conversion of pasture and row crops to vineyards. From 1992 to 2004, the acreage planted in vineyards within the approved Refuge boundary increased from 685 to 2,013 acres. The acreage of vineyards in Sacramento County nearly doubled from 1998 to 1999 (Sacramento County 1999, Sacramento County 2000). Whereas smaller vineyards interspersed with pasture, croplands and natural habitats can support a variety of wildlife, large expanses of vineyards provide little to no habitat for migratory birds and other wildlife.

Other Human Impacts
Air Quality

Poor air quality injures wildlife and vegetation, causes acidification of water, accelerates weathering of buildings and other facilities and impairs visibility. Air quality, and pollution control in particular, is regulated by a number of Federal and State agencies. Both the State of California and the Federal government have established a variety of ambient air quality standards. PM10 land ozone are two pollutants that are monitored and used to determine air quality on a daily basis. PM10 refers to particulate matter suspended in the air that is smaller than 10 microns, which are small enough to reach the lungs. Ozone is the main component of photochemical smog, which is formed through a series of chemical reactions involving compounds known as ozone precursors.

Sacramento County PM10 emissions are generated by a variety of sources, primarily entrained road dust, construction and demolition activities. Farming operations and agricultural waste burning are also important sources. Motor vehicles are the primary contributors to regional ozone concentrations because they are sources of ozone precursors. The U.S. EPA has declared that the Sacramento region is not meeting air quality standards. The Federal air quality standard for ozone is exceeded several times a year and the County has been classified as a PM10 nonattainment area (USEPA 2006).

Illegal Activity

The majority of illegal activities involve some sort of trespass by people or incursions by feral animals, such as cats and dogs. Trespass occurs in the form of walking, jogging, horseback riding,, hunting, fishing, and plant and material collecting. Trespassing results in poaching, wildlife disturbance, littering, vandalism and wildfires. Feral dogs and cats disturb and kill native wildlife and disturb cattle used to graze managed grasslands. Feral animal feces can also spread disease to native wildlife populations. Noxious weeds are spread when people and animals trespass into previously uninfested areas. Unwanted pets (rabbits, chickens, guinea pigs, dogs, cats) that are commonly released at entrances to the Refuge can cause similar problems.

Illegal dumping of both non-hazardous and hazardous materials (e.g., methamphetamine lab waste, pesticides, waste oil) near Refuge entrances presents an ongoing concern. Littering along Interstate-5, particular where commercial truck rigs make overnight rest stops (e.g., Hood-Franklin Road exit), has also become a significant problem as traffic increases on the interstate. The Refuge works with the County of Sacramento and the California Department of Transportation (Caltrans) to remove debris as quickly as possible but additional efforts and more cooperation are needed. Finally, arson-caused or accidental fires along Interstate-5 have become a serious management concern as the Refuge has expanded east of the freeway (i.e., Wetland Preserve Unit). As a result, the Refuge has pursued new partnership opportunities with the Elk Grove Community Services District under the Wildland Urban Interface program to create adequate firebreaks and ensure protection of adjacent communities such as the Stonelake subdivision.

Illegal dumping of both non-hazardous and hazardous materials inside and at the entrance gates to the Refuge is an obvious problem.
Photo by Tom Harvey, USFWS

More serious crimes, such as burglary and abandonment of burning stolen cars at more remote Refuge entrances, occur occasionally (one to two times per year). Marijuana gardens and evidence of other illegal drug activities have also been found. Illegal hunting and fishing occur most often along easy access points, such as roads or from private property.

Mosquito Management

In 1993, the Service and the Sacramento-Yolo Mosquito and Vector Control District entered into an MOU regarding management of mosquitos on the Refuge. The goal of the MOU is to minimize mosquito production and promote the least intrusive approaches to control mosquitos on the Refuge. The Refuge coordinates with SYMVCD in a variety of ways to minimize mosquito breeding habitat. For example, the Refuge staff ensure that wetlands are designed and water is manipulated in such a way to minimize mosquito production. The SYMVCD monitors wetlands on the Refuge and plants mosquito fish, when necessary, as an initial method of control. Alternately, if mosquito larvae are detected, Bti (*Bacillus thuringiensis israeliensis*) or *B. sphaericus* may be applied..

As a result, mosquito larval control activities since 1994 have been largely limited to localized (less than five acres) applications of larvicides and until 2005, and only three applications of an adulticides. In 2005, West Nile Virus (WNV) arrived and became established in Sacramento and Yolo counties, triggering more aggressive mosquito control. During 2005, the Refuge received ultra-low volume (ULV) ground treatments of pyrethrin on 18 occasions from September 28 through October 12. As of July 2006, the Refuge has been adulticided six times between June 27 and July 21.

Avian Bird Flu

To date, the virulent form of Highly Pathogenic Avian Influenza referred to as H5N1 has not been detected in either wild or domestic birds or in humans in North America. In fact, between 1998 and 2004 more than 12,000 wild bird samples from

Alaska were analyzed, and no evidence of this virus has been discovered, although birds migrating from Asia to Alaska could potentially carry the H5N1 virus.

The Service, U.S. Geological Survey (USGS), State and partnering academic institutions are continuing surveillance of wild birds in Alaska for the H5N1 virus. The Service is working with an interagency group of scientists and public health and policy officials to design an intensified effort for surveillance and early detection of this virus in wild birds. This effort will help ensure that the Service is in position to support prompt detection and response activities and to take appropriate measures to conserve bird populations while protecting the safety of employees, partners and the public.

The USGS National Wildlife Health Center, in consultation with the Centers for Disease Control and Prevention, has produced Wildlife Health Bulletin 05-03, entitled *Interim Guidelines for the Protection of Persons Handling Wild Birds With Reference to Highly Pathogenic Avian Influenza H5N1*. While reiterating that the H5N1 virus has not been detected in North America, these guidelines remind us of the importance of sensible safety practices. As the situation and information with regard to the H5N1 virus changes, these guidelines may be updated.

5 Refuge Vision, Goals, and Objectives

Vision Statement

"Stone Lakes National Wildlife Refuge belongs to a limited group among the 540 national wildlife refuges that protect fish, wildlife, and habitat within an urban area. Through collaboration with public and private partners, Stone Lakes conserves and enhances a range of scarce Sacramento-San Joaquin Delta and Central Valley habitats and the fish, wildlife, and plants they support. It sustains freshwater wetlands, wooded riparian corridors, and grasslands that facilitate wildlife movement and compensate for habitat fragmentation. Managed wetlands are of sufficient size to maintain abundant wildlife populations. Grasslands consist of a sustainable mix of native and desirable nonnative species that support a variety of grassland-dependent species. The Refuge reduces further habitat fragmentation and buffers the effects of urbanization on agricultural lands and adjacent natural areas within the Delta region.

The Refuge pursues a land conservation program that complements other regional efforts and initiatives. Management efforts expand and diversify habitats for migratory birds and a range of species at risk. The Refuge promotes cooperative farming opportunities and strives to maintain traditional agricultural practices in southwestern Sacramento County that have proven benefits for migratory birds experiencing declines, such as long-billed curlews, Swainson's hawks and sandhill cranes. Through cooperation with other agencies, conservation organizations, neighbors, and other partners, the Refuge develops and manages wetlands in a manner that reflects historic hydrologic patterns and is consistent with local, State, and Federal floodplain management goals and programs.

Volunteers from all walks of life find an outlet for their interests and talents in a responsive and appreciative setting.
Photo by USFWS

Stone Lakes was established as a national wildlife refuge because of passionate support from people who recognized its ecological importance and critical role for the floodplain of the Beach-Stone Lakes basin.. The community sees the Refuge as a sanctuary for fish, wildlife and the habitats upon which they depend, a site for recreation and learning and a natural setting that can enrich their lives according to their values. Visitors representing the area's diversity enjoy increasing opportunities for accessible recreation that harmonizes with Refuge conservation efforts, such as hunting, fishing, wildlife observation and photography. The education community looks to the Refuge as a key partner in environmental education programming. Volunteers from all walks of life find an outlet for their interests and talents in a responsive and appreciative setting."

Goals

Goals are descriptive, open-ended, and often broad statements of desired future conditions that convey a purpose but do not define measurable outcomes. Goals translate Refuge purposes into management direction. Each goal is supported by measurable, achievable objectives with specific strategies needed to accomplish them. Objectives are designed to be accomplished within 15 years. Actual implementation, however, may vary as a result of available funding or other resource limitations. Figures 6 and 7, respectively, show summaries of the proposed habitat management and visitor services plans for Stone Lakes National Wildlife Refuge.

Currently, the Service manages about 30 percent of the lands within the approved Refuge boundary. This CCP presents goals and objectives for only those lands that are or will soon be managed by the Service. The restoration objectives identified in this CCP are consistent with the restoration goals identified in Chapter 3B-3 of the 1992 Environmental Impact Statement (EIS) at the time of establishment of the approved Refuge boundary (USFWS 1992).

Goal 1. Conserve, enhance, restore and manage Central Valley wetland, riparian, grassland and other native habitats to benefit their associated fish, wildlife, plants and special status species.

Objective 1.A. Within 15 years, establish a minimum of 65 acres of valley foothill riparian and oak woodland habitat with a canopy cover of 20-80% and a canopy height of 2-10 meters. These newly planted habitats will have a complex structure with a canopy, subcanopy and understory shrub layer that will continue to mature beyond the lifetime of this CCP. An additional 40 acres of understory shrubs and herbaceous cover would be established in areas restored from 1995-1998. In the restored valley riparian habitats, wild grape will often cover trees and shrubs and will dominate 30 to 50 percent of the ground cover along with a shrub layer consisting of wild rose,

California blackberry, blue elderberry, poison oak, buttonbush and willows. The herbaceous layer will consist of various grasses and sedges. Dominant trees will include valley oak, cottonwood, California sycamore, white alder (Alnus rhombifolia), box elder and Oregon ash.

Rationale: Over 89 percent of the historic riparian woodland and 99 percent of oak savanna habitat in the Central Valley has been lost or converted since Euro-American settlement (DFG 2006). Refuge riparian habitat restoration efforts to date have produced approximately 107 acres of restored habitat, primarily on the Beach Lake Unit. Based on the riparian habitat restoration goals defined in the EIS (USFWS 1992), the Service intends to restore a minimum of 65 acres of additional riparian habitat over the next 15 years. Expanding riparian zones along lakes, sloughs and waterways will benefit a variety of species that use these habitats during migration, for nesting, feeding and roosting habitat. These restored habitats would provide breeding and migratory habitat for a variety of riparian dependent species which have been identified by the Central Valley Habitat Joint Venture as species of concern (G. Geupel, pers. comm.), including the yellow warbler, song sparrow, spotted towhee, yellow breasted chat, black headed grosbeak and common yellowthroat. Some of these species, extirpated locally or in severe decline, such as yellow warbler and yellow-breasted chat, would also benefit from restoration efforts. Understory shrub plantings that include elderberry bushes would benefit the Federally-listed valley elderberry longhorn beetle. Additionally, restoring riparian habitat will help achieve the conservation action recommendations set forth in the Riparian Bird Conservation Plan by the California Partners in Flight and the Riparian Habitat Joint Venture (RHJV 2004).

Strategies:
1. Restore and expand cottonwood riparian forest habitat along the south arm of North Stone Lake through planting and beaver exclusion fencing.

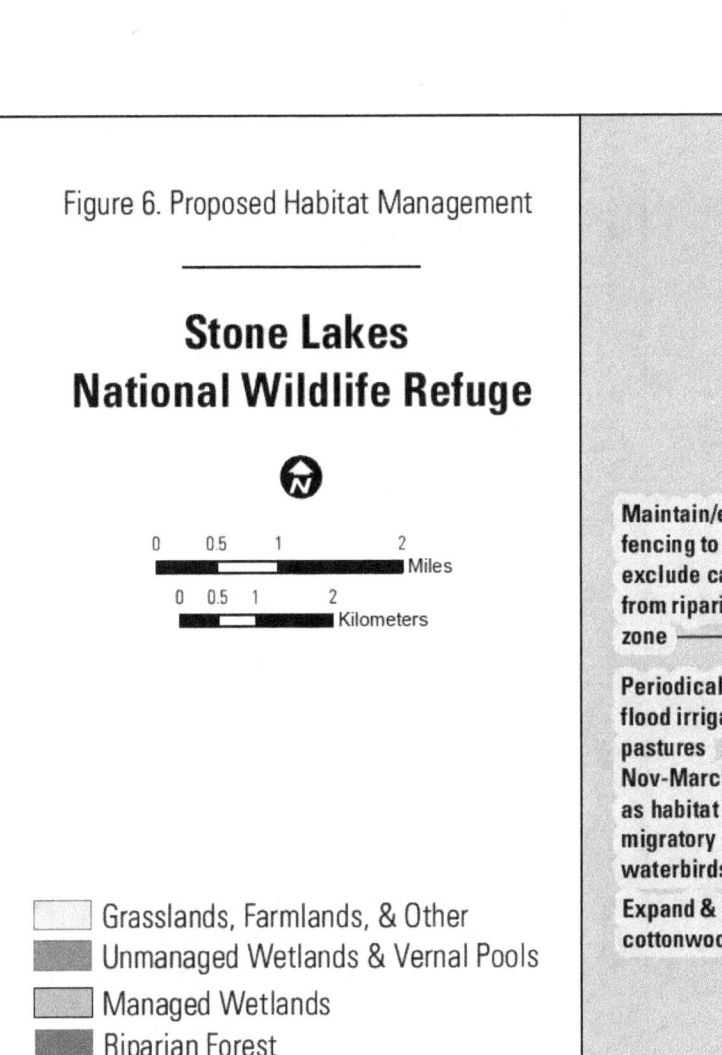

Figure 6. Proposed Habitat Management

Stone Lakes
National Wildlife Refuge

0   0.5   1   2
                                Miles

0   0.5   1   2
                      Kilometers

Grasslands, Farmlands, & Other
Unmanaged Wetlands & Vernal Pools
Managed Wetlands
Riparian Forest
Open Water
Non-Refuge Lands
Seasonally Flooded
Wetland Restoration
Riparian Restoration
Natural Riparian Expansion

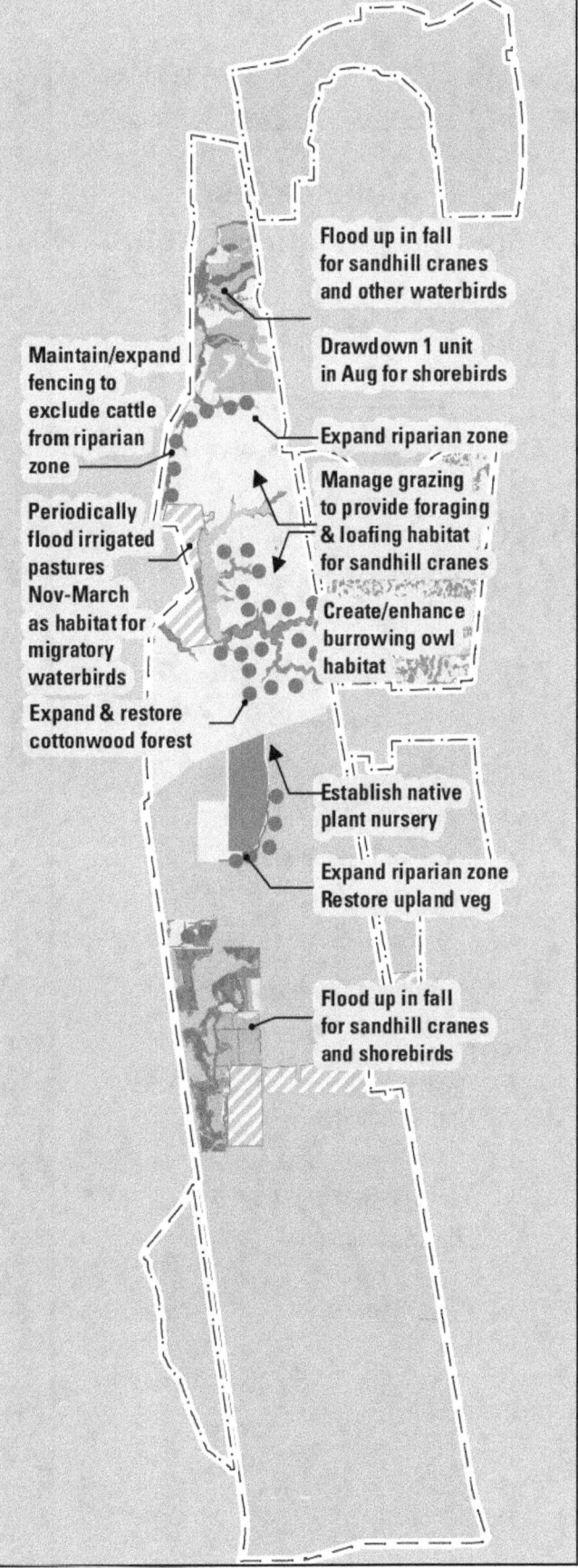

Flood up in fall for sandhill cranes and other waterbirds

Drawdown 1 unit in Aug for shorebirds

Maintain/expand fencing to exclude cattle from riparian zone

Expand riparian zone

Manage grazing to provide foraging & loafing habitat for sandhill cranes

Periodically flood irrigated pastures Nov-March as habitat for migratory waterbirds

Create/enhance burrowing owl habitat

Expand & restore cottonwood forest

Establish native plant nursery

Expand riparian zone Restore upland veg

Flood up in fall for sandhill cranes and shorebirds

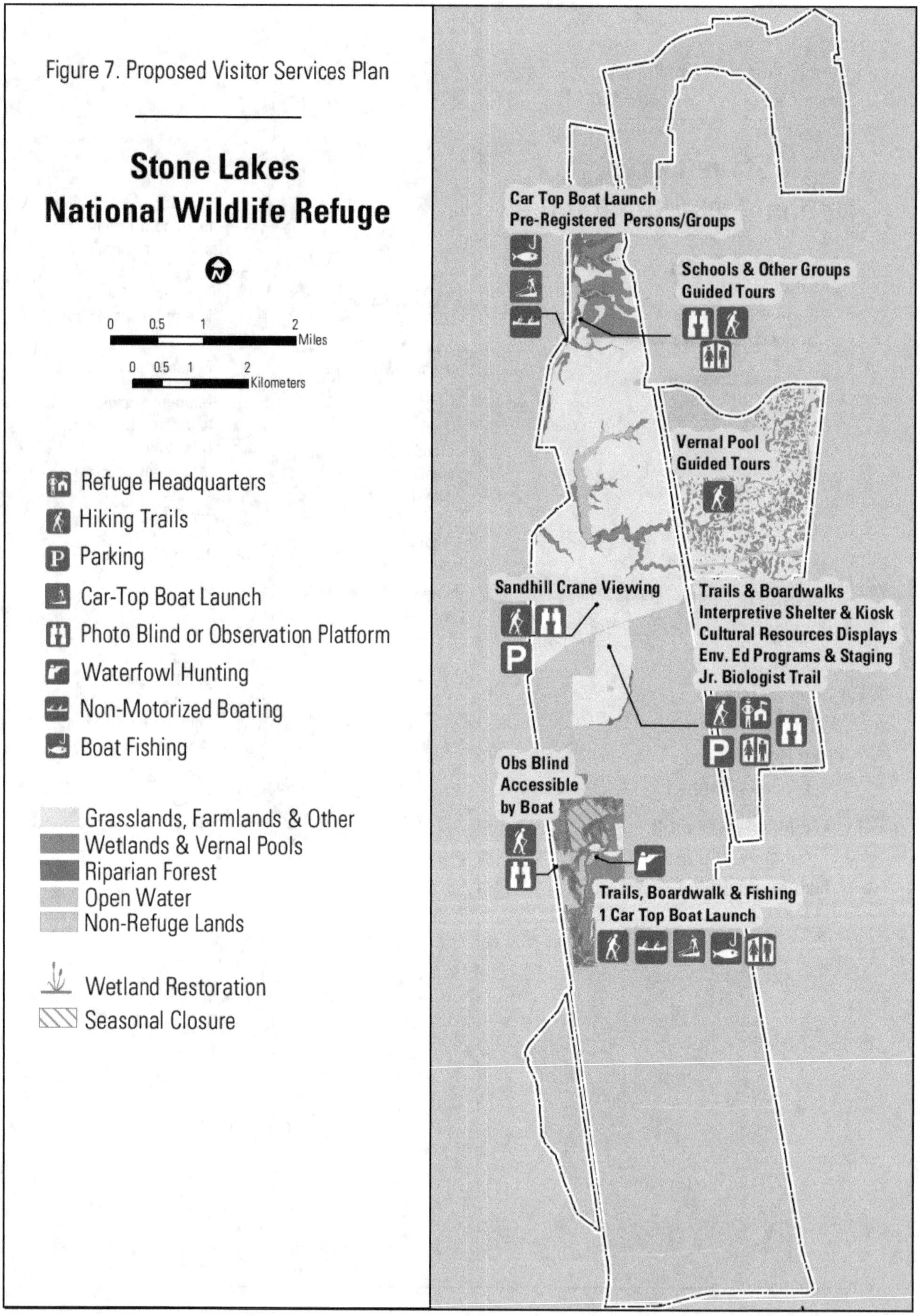

Figure 7. Proposed Visitor Services Plan

Stone Lakes
National Wildlife Refuge

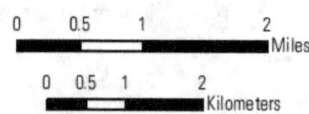

```
0    0.5   1           2
                         Miles
0    0.5   1           2
                         Kilometers
```

🏃	Refuge Headquarters
🚶	Hiking Trails
P	Parking
⛵	Car-Top Boat Launch
📷	Photo Blind or Observation Platform
🏹	Waterfowl Hunting
🛶	Non-Motorized Boating
🎣	Boat Fishing

Grasslands, Farmlands & Other
Wetlands & Vernal Pools
Riparian Forest
Open Water
Non-Refuge Lands

 Wetland Restoration
Seasonal Closure

Car Top Boat Launch
Pre-Registered Persons/Groups

Schools & Other Groups
Guided Tours

Vernal Pool
Guided Tours

Sandhill Crane Viewing

Trails & Boardwalks
Interpretive Shelter & Kiosk
Cultural Resources Displays
Env. Ed Programs & Staging
Jr. Biologist Trail

Obs Blind
Accessible
by Boat

Trails, Boardwalk & Fishing
1 Car Top Boat Launch

2. Expand the riparian zone to a range of 150 to 400 feet wide along the Sacramento Drainage Canal of the South Stone Lake and Headquarters Units.
3. Restore approximately 20 acres to a combination of native trees, shrubs, and grasses on the upland areas of the Headquarters Unit.
4. Establish/enhance subcanopy and understory in new and established riparian habitat areas on the Beach Lake and North Stone Lake units.
5. Establish native plant nursery at the Headquarters Unit for use in restoration projects.
6. Plant early to mid-successional vegetation on the western portion of the Lewis Investment Co. tract of the South Stone Lake Unit.
7. Assist the Sacramento Regional County Sanitation District in expanding the valley oak forest along lower Morrison Creek on the CAMRAY tract of the Beach Lake Unit by seeking funding and other support for restoration.
8. Allow expansion of riparian habitat along existing riparian corridors including managed seasonal wetlands.
9. Identify and map weed infestations, track assessments and treatments and produce maps and reports that can be shared with other interested parties.
10. Intensify control efforts for perennial pepperweed in riparian areas using a variety of methods including pesticides, mowing, and hand-pulling.
11. Cooperate with U.S. Department of Agriculture (USDA) and local academic institutions to research new methods for controlling invasive plants.
12. Measure habitat characteristics (e.g., canopy cover, species composition) of riparian plantings in areas with a high diversity of bird species, as indicated by mist netting data collected over the past six years on Lewis unit, to guide future restoration efforts.

Objective 1.B: Maintain and manage on an annual basis 425 acres of riparian and oak woodland habitat, consisting of 360 acres of existing habitat and 65 acres of restored habitat (See Objective 1.A). This

habitat encompasses riparian and oak woodland habitat in various successional stages comprising a complex structure with a canopy, sub-canopy, and understory shrub layer (usually impenetrable). Restoration would occur through habitat manipulations, including control of invasive plant species and restoration of the sub-canopy and understory shrub layer by planting native species. Wild grape often covers trees and shrubs and dominates the ground cover along with a shrub layer consisting of wild rose, California blackberry, blue elderberry, poison oak, buttonbush and willows. The herbaceous layer consists of various grasses and sedges. Dominant trees include valley oak, cottonwood, California sycamore, white alder, box elder and Oregon ash.

Rationale: Valley foothill riparian habitats occur in the Central Valley and the lower foothills of the Sierra Nevada and Coast Ranges and are associated with low velocity flows, floodplains and gentle topography. Over 89 percent of the historic riparian woodland and 99 percent of oak savanna habitat in the Central Valley has been lost or converted since Euro-American settlement (DFG 2006). These habitats comprise a complex structure with a canopy, subcanopy and understory shrub layer. Based on the population trends and life history requirements of various species in the Central Valley, the Central Valley Habitat Joint Venture has developed a list of focal migratory bird species that can be used to guide restoration and management efforts. Riparian habitats provide breeding and migratory habitat for the following focal species for the Central Valley, as defined by the Central Valley Habitat Joint Venture (G. Geupel, PRBO, pers. comm.): yellow warbler, song sparrow, spotted towhee, yellow breasted chat, black headed grosbeak and common yellowthroat. Furthermore, these riparian areas support heron and egret rookeries that vary in size from ten to 50 nests. The bird species previously listed and others, use a variety of successional stages within riparian habitat. Maintaining and managing high quality riparian habitat, in various successional stages, will help achieve the conservation action recommendations set forth in the Riparian Bird Conservation Plan (RHJV 2004).

Strategies:
1. Monitor riparian and oak woodland habitats each spring for invasive species such as perennial pepperweed and yellow star thistle and implement control methods based on integrated pest management techniques, including herbicide applications and grazing (see Objective 1.A).
2. Monitor riparian areas for existing and newly-established heron and egret rookeries (See Strategy 2.B.2).
3. Maintain and expand fencing along SP Cut on the North Stone Lake Unit to exclude cattle from riparian areas.
4. Conduct annual surveys of riparian habitats for damage by beavers, research methods to discourage beavers, and implement protection measures (e.g., wrapping trees with hog wire or fencing).

Objective 1.C: **Within five years, enhance and maintain approximately 50 acres of seasonal and permanent wetlands created on the 70 acre Lewis Investment Co. tract of the South Stone Lake Unit by promoting growth of wetland species such as swamp timothy, smartweeds, watergrass and associated invertebrates. These wetland species provide food for waterfowl and other waterbirds.**

Rationale: Approximately 95 percent of wetlands in the Central Valley have been lost or converted to other land uses (DFG 2006). Improving water management on the Lewis Investment Co. tract would reverse some of these losses and benefit a wide variety of migratory birds and other wildlife, including special status species, such as giant garter snake, western pond turtle, white-faced ibis, greater sandhill crane, long-billed curlew, black-bellied plover, black-necked stilt and long-billed dowitcher (*Limnodromus scolopaceus*) and help achieve CVJV goals.

Strategies:
1. Modify existing water delivery system on the South Stone Lake Unit to deliver water to the Lewis Investment Co. Tract.
2. Control undesirable vegetation using a combinations of the following treatments: mowing, discing, burning, herbicide applications and summer flooding.
3. Explore the possibility of applying reverse-cycle water management on an experimental basis to benefit shorebirds.

Objective 1.D: **Manage on an annual basis 529 acres as moist soil habitat, characterized by a plant composition of 50 percent or more moist soil, high-energy waterfowl plant foods including: watergrass, swamp timothy and smartweeds. Flood approximately 60 percent of the moist soil units to a depth of 2 to 10 inches for dabbling ducks and shorebirds and 40 percent to depths of 6 inches to 3 feet for diving ducks, grebes, cormorants, pelicans, waders and other waterbirds.**

Rationale: All managed seasonal wetlands on the Refuge consist of moist soil impoundments which support a wide variety of waterbirds, with peak numbers of waterfowl and shorebirds occurring in the late fall and winter. Species groups having varying requirements for vegetation and water depth. For example, dabbling ducks, such as cinnamon and green winged teal, mallard and northern pintail prefer to feed in shallow water, with an equal ratio of open water and emergent vegetation, whereas diving ducks, such as bufflehead (*Bucephala albeola*), canvasback and common goldeneye (*Bucephala clangula*) prefer deeper water. Shorebirds, such as long-billed dowitcher, black-bellied plover, and black-necked stilts, feed on mudflats or in shallow water of varying depths, depending on species. Managed seasonal wetlands on the Refuge are currently operated under a fall-migration-oriented regime with flood-up from mid-September or October through May, which optimizes habitat availability for fall migrants. Flooding seasonal wetlands under a reverse-cycle regime from March through August could provide late winter food before migration and habitat for breeding shorebirds and waterfowl broods. Species supported by this objective include special status species such as white-faced ibis and greater sandhill crane.

Strategies:
1. Flood moist soil wetland impoundments, depending on water availability, on Beach Lake and South Stone Lake units starting September 1 and no later than mid-September and maintain through March to May for migratory and wintering waterbirds, including waterfowl, shorebirds and sandhill cranes.
2. Stagger the timing of drawdown for moist soil units beginning in March.
3. Irrigate units one or two times from May through August to promote waterfowl food such as watergrass and swamp timothy
4. Disc and/or mow 25-50 percent of the units to stimulate growth of waterfowl food plants and mow or disc to maintain an equal ratio of open water to emergent vegetation.
5. Control undesirable plants such as cocklebur and joint grass using one or more of the following treatments: mowing, discing, burning, herbicide applications, or summer flooding.
6. Explore the possibility of applying reverse-cycle water management on an experimental basis to benefit shorebirds.
7. Draw down one permanent wetland unit beginning in August to provide habitat for migrating shorebirds. Flood the unit again in late September, when other wetlands are being flooded.

Objective 1.E: Maintain 452 acres annually of unmanaged seasonal wetlands (i.e., wetlands with no capability to manipulate water regimes) so they support 50 percent or more moist soil, high energy waterfowl plant foods, including watergrass, swamp timothy, and smartweeds, interspersed with open water while controlling undesirable vegetation, such as cocklebur, yellow star thistle and perennial pepperweed to benefit wintering and migratory waterfowl, as well as other wetland-dependent species.

Rationale: Unmanaged seasonal wetlands with no capability for water manipulations are found on all units of the Refuge. These wetlands receive water passively from rain and runoff only and are typically dry during summer. Once flooded, these wetlands attract a variety of waterbirds such as cinnamon teal, northern pintail, white-fronted goose, black-bellied plover, black necked stilt, long-billed dowitcher, sandhill crane and long-billed curlew.

Strategies:
1. Monitor unmanaged wetlands each spring for undesirable vegetation such as cocklebur and other noxious weeds such as yellow star thistle and perennial pepperweed and implement control methods as needed.
2. Use burning, grazing, discing, mowing and/or herbicide application to control the growth of invasive species and promote the growth of desirable wetland plants, such as watergrass, swamp timothy, smartweeds and nutsedges, in seasonal swales.

Objective 1.F: Annually maintain 136 acres of vernal pool seasonal wetlands characterized by greater than 70 percent native vernal pool vegetation.

Rationale: Vernal pool habitats support a variety of vernal pool species, including the federally endangered vernal pool fairy shrimp and vernal pool tadpole shrimp, as well as various species of special concern, including vernal pool plant species (USFWS 2006). These pools are best managed through prescribed grazing from November through June. Without grazing, a dense layer of nonnative annual grasses can exclude native vernal pool plants and consume water to the extent that vernal pools become prematurely dry. Grazing reduces the competitiveness of native plants versus nonnative plants, and may prolong inundation of vernal pools in the spring (J. Marty, TNC, pers. comm.).

Strategies:
1. Monitor wetlands each spring for undesirable vegetation, such as cocklebur, and noxious weeds, such

as yellow starthistle and perennial pepperweed and implement control efforts as needed.

2. In cooperation with the landowner, develop a grazing management plan for the Wetland Preserve Unit that maintains a residual dry matter level, as measured in August through September, of 800-1000 lbs/acre.

3. Depending on air quality regulatory restrictions, employ prescribed burns to reduce nonnative annual grasses and replicate the historical fire regime as closely as possible.

4. Develop proposals and support research to characterize plant and animal communities in natural versus created vernal pools.

Objective 1.G: Annually maintain 715 acres of deep water wetlands (including wetlands with and without a capability to manipulate water regimes), lakes, sloughs and SP Cut to provide breeding, foraging and loafing habitat for waterfowl and other wetland dependent species, such as giant garter snakes and western pond turtles. Deep water wetlands will be characterized by water depths of greater than three feet supporting wetland plants species such as tules, cattails, burreed (Sparganium spp.) and water primrose. Wetlands with the capability to manipulate water regimes (106 acres) will be managed to support a 50:50 ratio of tall emergent vegetation to open water.

Rationale: Permanent wetlands include wetlands, lakes, sloughs and waterways with different water management capabilities. Deeper water habitats interspersed with tall emergent vegetation, such as cattails and tules, provide excellent habitat for a variety of migrating, wintering and resident birds, including special status species, such as greater white-fronted geese, canvasbacks, northern pintails, wood ducks, common moorhens, American bitterns, American white pelicans and pied-billed grebes. An approximately equal percentage of open water for foraging and tall emergent vegetation for cover provides an optimal mix of habitat types. Riparian habitats

associated with these wetlands may support colonies of nesting great blue herons, great egrets, double-crested cormorants, black-crowned night herons, and snowy egrets and a variety of raptors such as the Swainson's hawk. Fallen trees and logs provide basking sites for species such as western pond turtles and permanent wetlands, sloughs and waterways provide habitat for the endangered giant garter snake. Many of these wetlands were degraded through dredging, farming and other activities and are currently further threatened by degradation of water quality and invasive aquatic weeds such as water hyacinth.

Strategies:
1. Reduce human disturbances to nesting birds and other wildlife on deep water habitats such as lakes, sloughs and the SP Cut by limiting public access.

2. Continue to work in partnership with private landowners and local and State agencies and academic institutions to control water hyacinth and participate in the Stone Lakes Basin Water Hyacinth Control Program.

3. Within five years, survey aquatic plants in South Stone Lake and map distribution of Brazilian elodea and other non native plants to determine if control efforts are needed and if so, what methods can be used .

4. Cooperate with the U.S. Department of Agriculture and local academic institutions on evaluating alternate, nonchemical methods of controlling invasive weeds.

5. Assess necessity and feasibility of drawing down North Stone Lake to solidify a portion of the bottom of the lake to stimulate plant growth.

6. Maintain approximately an equal ratio of emergent vegetation to open water on the Beach Lake and South Stone Lake units through a combination of drawdowns, mowing, discing and prescribed burning in sloughs.

7. Drawdown managed permanent wetlands every two to four years to control carp populations and improve germination of desirable wetland plants..

8. Maintain sanctuary areas for nesting waterbirds, (e.g., pied-billed grebes) waterfowl broods, giant garter snakes, and western pond turtle from May through September in the central portion of South Stone Lake (see Figure 6).

Objective 1.H: Manage and enhance approximately 1,900 acres of non-irrigated grasslands on the North Stone Lake Unit on an annual basis to provide a variety of grass heights and densities as measured by residual dry matter (RDM) at the end of the grazing season, which is typically November to June depending primarily on precipitation and other factors. Pasture rotation reduces grazing pressure on different pasture units and promotes a diversity of grassland-dependent species, such as arctic nesting geese, shorebirds, songbirds, burrowing owl and other raptors, sandhill crane and long-billed curlew which have been identified by the Service as focal species.

Rationale: Over 99.9 percent of historic native grasslands in the Central Valley have been lost to agricultural conversion and urban development since Euro-American settlement (DFG 2006). The large ungulates, pronghorn antelope and tule elk, that once grazed these grasslands were extirpated from the valley by the 1870s. The natural hydrologic regime of the area has also been irreversibly modified. Despite these changes, the 2,600-acre North Stone Lake Unit is one of the largest and relatively unaltered grassland areas left in the Stone Lakes Basin. It supports a variety of special status species, such as the greater sandhill crane, burrowing owl, Swainson's hawk, California horned lark, long-billed curlew and western meadowlark. Since grazing was reintroduced following a ten-year absence, many of the species mentioned above expanded their use of the Refuge.

Strategies:
1. Graze cattle on the North Stone Lake Unit from November 1 to July 15; actual termination dates will vary from year to year depending on rainfall and grass production.

2. Use integrated pest management techniques, including prescribed fire, mowing, discing, hand removal and herbicide applications, to reduce invasive plants, such as yellow starthistle, pepperweed and other undesirable grassland vegetation.

3. Implement a long term grazing management plan developed in collaboration with USDA Natural Resource Conservation Service (NRCS) and other range management experts. The plan prescribes stocking rates to achieve varying grass heights and densities in the five pastures of the unit to accommodate habitat requirements of breeding and wintering bird species, including sandhill cranes, long-billed curlews and western meadowlarks. The overall goal is to annually rotate grazing pressure (e.g., low, medium or high) among the five pastures, resulting in a range of grass heights and densities. Two pastures will be maintained with relatively lower residual dry matter (RDM) values as measured at the end of the grazing season (1,200 lbs/acre), two pastures with medium RDM values (1,750 lbs/acre) and one pasture with a higher RDM value (+2,500 lbs/acre). .

4. Enhance and create habitat for burrowing owls by reintroducing ground squirrels to the North Stone Lake Unit and constructing and maintaining artificial burrows until sufficient natural burrows are available.

5. Develop long term monitoring plan to survey population trends of greater sandhill cranes, arctic nesting geese, long-billed curlews, white-faced ibis, burrowing owls, and western meadowlarks to evaluate wildlife responses to range management.

6. Develop methodologies to restore native grasses on the North Stone Lakes Unit through test plots in conjunction with USDA NRCS and Agriculture Plant Material Center.

Objective 1.I: *Annually maintain 460 acres of irrigated pasture/wet meadow to provide habitat for a variety of grassland dependent species, including sandhill cranes, white faced ibis, long-billed curlew and arctic nesting geese.*

Rationale: With less than one percent of native grasslands left in the Central Valley, many grassland dependent species now rely on dry and irrigated pastures for migrating and wintering habitat. Irrigated pastures on the North Stone Lake Unit support the largest concentration of native grasses on the Refuge. Irrigated pasture is sheet-flooded in winter to bring invertebrates to the surface, providing foraging habitat for cranes and shorebirds.

Strategies:
1. Continue irrigation of 460 acres of pastures on the North Stone Lake and South Stone Lake units and the Gallagher tract from June through October.
2. If feasible, sheet flood irrigated pastures to a depth of less than six inches every two weeks from November through March on the North Stone Lake Unit (also see 2.A.2).
3. Provide short grass habitat through a managed grazing program from July through October.
4. Develop a monitoring plan to survey native grasses and develop mapping capabilities and strategies to expand native grasses.

Objective 1.J: *Restore approximately 30 acres to grassland habitat consisting of a minimum of 70 percent native grasses including; needlegrass, bluegrass (Poa spp.), rye grass, Elymus spp., and Melica spp. on various Refuge units within 10 years to promote biodiversity and improve the grassland communities on the Refuge.*

Rationale: Native grasses once covered nearly 22 million acres of California, including much of the Central Valley (Heady 1977). Today, over 99.9 percent of these grasslands have been lost (DFG 2006). Although little is known about the original composition of native grasses of the Stone Lakes Basin, purple needlegrass may have dominated the valley grasslands with a mix of other perennial grasses, including bluegrass, rye grass, *Elymus* spp. and *Mellica* spp.; annual grasses such as Fescue (*Festuca* spp.); and a mixture of broad-leaved forbs (Heady 1977; Stebbins 1965). Because little is known about the original composition of the grasses and dramatic changes in land use and hydrology have occurred, local experts are the best source of information when planning native grassland restorations.

Strategies:
1. Establish small (less than 0.25 acre) experimental native grass plots before large scale restoration activities are conducted.
2. Remove nonnative seed sources by mowing, discing, burning, or chemical applications for two seasons before establishing native grasses and control broadleaves and other invasive plants on newly restored areas for three years or more.
3. Maintain grasslands by periodic disturbance, such as mowing, grazing, burning, or discing outside of the breeding season for birds.
4. Use local expertise in developing native grassland restoration plans.
5. Restore 3-5 acres of the western portion of the Lewis Investment Co. tract of the South Stone Lake Unit to a grassland community with an objective of 60 percent native grasses through discing, seeding, mowing and herbicide applications outside of the breeding season for birds.
6. Develop a monitoring plan to assess the success of native grass restoration projects.

Objective 1.K: *Within 15 years, coordinate the Refuge land conservation program to protect 75 percent of the land within the approved Refuge boundary to help achieve the Central Valley Joint Venture (CVJV) regional habitat protection goals.*

Rationale: One of the goals identified in the EIS that established the approved Refuge boundary (USFWS 1992), is creating linkages between Refuge habitats and habitats on adjacent lands to reverse the impacts of past habitat fragmentation on wildlife and plants. Therefore, priority should be given to conserving lands within the approved Refuge boundary and coordinating Refuge land conservation activities with other nearby regional conservation projects to compensate for habitat fragmentation caused by agricultural conversion and urban development. The CVJV is a partnership of conservation organizations and State and Federal agencies whose mission is to work collaboratively through diverse partnerships to protect, restore and enhance wetlands and associated habitats for waterfowl, shorebirds, waterbirds and riparian songbirds, in accordance with conservation actions identified in the CVJV Implementation Plan. Through these actions, the CVJV aims to advance its vision of providing diverse habitats necessary to sustain migratory bird populations in perpetuity for the benefit of those species, resident wildlife and the public. The Central Valley of California is the most important waterfowl wintering area in the Pacific Flyway, supporting 60 percent of the total duck and goose population. In its implementation plan, the CVJV sets out habitat protection, enhancement and restoration objectives for sub-basin of the Central Valley, including the Sacramento San Joaquin Delta.

Strategies:
1. Coordinate Refuge land conservation activities with local and State agencies and private organizations, including the Sacramento Regional County Sanitation District, Sacramento County Department of Regional Parks, Recreation and Open Space, California Department of Parks and Recreation, California Department of Water Resources, The Nature Conservancy, the Trust for Public Land and the American Land Conservancy.
2. Continue to seek congressionally-appropriated funds (including Land and Water Conservation Funds and Migratory Bird Conservation Funds) and other Federal, State and private funding for land conservation.
3. Acquire agricultural and conservation easements on farmland and other fish and wildlife habitats within the approved Refuge boundary.
4. Participate actively in regional land planning efforts by Sacramento County, Cities of Elk Grove and Sacramento, Sacramento Area Council of Governments, and others that may promote the maintenance of open space and wildlife corridors between the Refuge and other regional open space areas.
5. Within one year, complete conveyance of fee title interest in the 150-acre Beach Lake Mitigation Bank (Beach Lake Unit) from California Department of Transportation.
6. Within two years, finalize a cooperative agreement with the Sacramento Regional County Sanitation District for joint management of the 1,800 acres of the Sacramento Regional Wastewater Treatment Plant Bufferlands lying within the approved Refuge boundary.
7. Within 15 years, secure funding to protect 75 percent of land with the approved Refuge boundary by working with willing landowners.

Objective 1.L: Coordinate Refuge habitat conservation efforts with other private and public conservation efforts within the Sacramento-San Joaquin Delta to contribute to regional habitat conservation needs.

Rationale: The EIS establishing the approved Refuge boundary (USFWS 1992) identified two goals: (1) coordinate Refuge land acquisition and management activities with other agencies and organizations to maximize the effectiveness of Refuge contributions to regional habitat needs, and (2) preserve, enhance, and restore Central Valley wetlands and agricultural lands to provide foraging and sanctuary habitat to achieve distribution and population levels of migratory waterbirds consistent with goals and objectives of the Central Valley Joint Venture (CVJV). Therefore, coordination of the conservation efforts of various management entities should support a greater diversity of fish and wildlife values and recreational opportunities. Under the North American Waterfowl Management Plan, the CVJV was established for habitat conservation and management of migratory waterbirds in the Central Valley. Current CVJV habitat objectives for the Sacramento-San Joaquin Delta to which the Refuge may contribute include: (1) restore 19,000 acres of wetlands; (2) enhance 2,112 acres of wetlands; and (3) enhance 23,000 acres of agricultural land. The Service would coordinate efforts with ongoing private and public conservation projects, including the CVJV, Riparian Habitat Joint Venture, Cosumnes River Preserve, Yolo Basin Wildlife Area, Delta Meadows State Park and other State-owned Delta properties.

Strategies:
1. Within three years, modify the existing cooperative agreement with Sacramento County Department of Regional Parks, Recreation and Open Space for their 1,567-acre portion of the North Stone Lake Unit so the agreement has a 30-year duration, and includes the habitat and visitor use strategies outlined in the CCP and Sacramento County's revised Draft North Stone Lake Management and Restoration Plan.
2. Within three years, secure long term management through cooperative agreement of the California Department of Parks and Recreation 1,224-acre portion of the North Stone Lake Unit.
3. Within five years, develop a cooperative agreement with California Department of Water Resources for joint management of the 410 acres they own within the approved Refuge boundary.
4. Pursue inclusion of the Service as a signatory to the joint operating agreement for the Cosumnes River Preserve to support the conservation and management of lands within and adjacent to the approved Refuge boundary.

5. In cooperation with the Natural Resources Conservation Service (NRCS) and other agencies and private organizations, pursue enhancement of privately-owned lands within and outside of the approved Refuge boundary by working with landowners through various programs, such as Partners for Fish and Wildlife and NRCS programs (e.g., Conservation Reserve Enhancement Program, Environmental Quality Incentives Program, and Wildlife Habitat Incentives Program).
6. Continue to participate actively in regional land use planning by State, county and municipal entities that may affect Refuge resources or complement Refuge conservation goals (see also 1.M).

Objective 1.M: Manage Refuge floodplain lands in a manner consistent with local, State and Federal flood management, sediment and erosion control and water quality objectives as described in the Environmental Impact Statement (EIS) establishing the approved Refuge boundary.

Rationale: The importance of the Beach-Stone Lakes Basin as a flood storage area during winter high flow events continues to increase with upstream urban development. The resulting changes in the flooding regime have also reduced the viability of some agricultural operations and modified patterns of remaining natural vegetation. In the EIS that established the approved Refuge boundary (USFWS 1992), the Service recognized flood storage as an important benefit and natural component of the Beach Stone Lakes ecosystem. Refuge restoration and management will be consistent with Federal, State and local flood guidelines.

Strategies:
1. Participate in regional interagency floodplain management planning efforts that may affect the Beach-Stone Lakes Basin, including the North Delta Improvement Group, Lower Morrison Creek planning, Mokelumne-Cosumnes Watershed Alliance, Pt. Pleasant Flood

Control Working Group and Sacramento River Planning Forum.

2. Implement Refuge habitat improvement strategies so that they do not exacerbate local or regional flooding, degrade water quality, or cause erosion impacts for adjacent or nearby landowners or residents.

3. Review and participate in regional planning activities sponsored by Sacramento County and local municipalities, such as the City of Elk Grove, which may affect flooding regimes or water quality in the Beach-Stone Lakes Basin.

4. Develop a Refuge levee flood control channel maintenance MOU in coordination with local agencies, such as reclamation and resource conservation districts, the City of Elk Grove, and Sacramento County, that is consistent with existing or future flood control policies.

Objective 1.N: *Within 10 years of CCP approval, work toward achieving the water quality supply standard for wetlands and fish and wildlife resources set forth by the U.S. Environmental Protection Agency (USEPA), the California Department of Fish and Game (DFG) and the Regional Water Quality Control Board.*

Rationale: Establishing a water quality monitoring program was recommended as a mitigation measure in the EIS establishing the approved Refuge boundary (USFWS 1992) and as part of subsequent water quality investigations (Thomas 2003). A water quality monitoring program can be used to further education and outreach efforts to local landowners, businesses and agricultural landowners, and can inform regulatory activity, if needed. Current threats to Refuge water quality include: eutrophic conditions (excess nutrients), turbidity, low dissolved oxygen, contaminants in urban and agricultural runoff (e.g., polycyclic aromatic hydrocarbons (PAHs), fecal coliform and pesticides) as well as mercury from historic mining operations.

Two options exist for the Refuge to comply with the Central Valley Regional Water Quality Control Board's (Regional Board) Irrigated Lands Conditional Waiver for water dischargers: filing as an individual discharger; or joining a discharge Coalition Group. Discharges from the Refuge into Waters of the State are not a regular occurrence and only occur periodically during flood events in which most of the flood water stays on Refuge lands and is not discharged. In addition the Refuge cooperates with the SRCSD Bufferlands staff to collect and analyze water samples to assess any impacts resulting from the application of aquatic herbicides. Previously the Refuge complied with water quality testing, to assess any concentration of aquatic herbicides, in compliance with the California Department of Boating and Waterways National Pollution Discharge Elimination System (NPDES) permit. Given that minimal discharge, if any, occurs from the Refuge and that water quality monitoring is already occurring, the Refuge will file as an individual discharger, or as a Coalition Group Member if appropriate.

To comply with the Irrigated Lands Conditional Waiver as an Individual discharger, the Refuge must file a Notice of Intent (NOI) to comply and a Farm Evaluation Report. Additional required reports will include a Monitoring and Report Program Plan and water quality monitoring, evaluated in a complete annual report to the Regional Water Board. In addition, technical reports may also be required, by the Regional Board, should water quality problems occur. The requirements for those that join a Coalition Group and file under the Conditional Waiver for Coalition Groups are identical except that a Watershed Evaluation Report is required in place of a Farm Evaluation Report. The reports required from the Coalition Groups include the filing of a NOI and General Report, Monitoring and Reporting Program Plan, Annual Monitoring Reports and the potential for a development of a Management Plan if required to resolve exceedance of water quality objectives.

Strategies:

1. Work to ensure coverage under the Central Valley Regional Water Quality Control Board Irrigated Lands Conditional Waiver, either as an Individual discharger or as a Coalition Group member if appropriate.
2. Develop a Refuge water quality monitoring program to track changes in contaminant concentrations, and water quality parameters (pH and dissolved oxygen) resulting from current and future land use patterns around the Refuge within five years.
3. Develop a long-term water quality monitoring program to assess the effects of non-point sources of pollution (including stormwater and agriculture runoff) entering the Refuge and the contaminant levels in fish and other biota.
4. Develop strategies to work with local landowners, businesses and neighborhood organizations within the watershed to educate and reduce quantities of pesticides and runoff entering the Refuge.
5. Expand the Refuge outreach and education effort to inform upstream urban residents and businesses of the sensitivity of downstream water uses.
6. Develop a partnership with Franklin High School to monitor water quality on the Refuge.

Goal 2. Conserve, enhance, and restore high quality migrating, wintering and breeding habitat for migratory birds within the Sacramento San Joaquin Delta of the Central Valley.

Objective 2.A: Manage 2,950 acres of Refuge lands and cooperate with nearby farmers and landowners to conserve and enhance agricultural lands and habitats that support 400-700 greater and lesser sandhill cranes wintering in the Stone Lakes Basin. The Refuge will continue management of seasonal wetlands and irrigated pasture to provide roosting and foraging habitat and pursuing projects and partnerships to maintain dry and irrigated pastures, wheat, corn, and alfalfa for cranes foraging in the basin.

Rationale: The greater sandhill crane is listed by the State as a threatened subspecies, under the California Endangered Species Act (CESA). Cranes winter in the Central Valley and depend on a combination of agricultural lands, wetlands and pasture. As urban expansion and conversion of agricultural crops and pastures to vineyards continues, habitat availability for cranes has decreased. Winter home ranges for greater sandhill cranes are relatively small, averaging less than one square mile, despite fluctuating food availability during the winter season (G. Ivey, pers. comm.). Nightly roost sites need to be in close proximity (less than one mile) to feeding sites. The Refuge can play an important role in the recovery of this subspecies by providing winter roosting and foraging habitat to support approximately 200 to 300 greater sandhill cranes near the North and South Stone Lake units and the surrounding area.

Strategies:

1. Begin flood up of seasonal and permanent wetlands on the Beach Lake and South Stone Lake units in early September to provide habitat for arriving (migrating) cranes, particularly when roosting habitat in the area is in short supply.
2. Periodically sheet-flood irrigated pastures in winter to provide foraging opportunities on the North Stone Lake Unit.
3. Continue grazing the North Stone Lake Unit to provide foraging and loafing habitat adjacent to roosting sites in wetlands (see objective 1.F).
4. Develop and host workshops to provide private landowners with information about USDA, NRCS and other Federal, State and private grant and incentive programs aimed at maintaining small grain fields for crane forage and protecting or enhancing other habitats important for wintering crane within a five-mile radius of the Refuge.
5. Maintain 40 to 60 acres of agriculture fields on the Headquarters Unit of the Refuge for foraging cranes. Crops could include corn, winter wheat and other small grains.

6. Conduct bimonthly sandhill crane surveys and coordinate results with appropriate researchers and refuges including the Cosumnes River Preserve and Modoc and Malheur national wildlife refuges.

7. Incorporate crane roosting habitat characteristics (e.g., shallow water, small islands with gravel, and minimizing human disturbance) into any new wetland development plans.

Objective 2.B: Develop monitoring strategies for focal species identified in various regional bird conservation plans to assess current and guide future habitat restoration activities. The regional plans include: the Central Valley Joint Venture Implementation Plan, the Riparian Bird Conservation Plan, the Grassland Bird Conservation Plan, the Oak Woodland Bird Conservation Plan, the North American Waterbird Conservation Plan, the North American Waterfowl Management Plan, and the North American Landbird Conservation Plan.

Rationale: Population monitoring and research assessing the habitat requirements of migratory birds is needed to evaluate the effectiveness of Refuge management strategies and facilitate adaptive management. Monitoring and research on the Refuge, in cooperation with other similar efforts in the Central Valley, will provide valuable information about population trends and assist with development of overall strategies for the recovery and management of migratory birds and other key species groups. Collaborative efforts between the Refuge and other agencies, academic institutions, and private organizations will increase the effectiveness of data collection efforts, expand the resources available and enable the Service to address a larger array of research and monitoring needs.

The Sacramento-Yolo Mosquito and Vector Control District (SYMVCD) has monitored landbirds on the Refuge weekly through mist netting and banding since 1995. The program has assisted the Service with assessing the quality of Refuge riparian habitats and avian species diversity. The goals of this program are to: assess the role of wild birds as reservoirs for mosquito-borne diseases such as Western Equine Encephalitis, St. Louis Encephalitis, and West Nile virus; assess the usefulness of bird populations as an early warning system for potential viral episodes; and provide information regarding species diversity, population status, seasonal use and reproductive success and recruitment on the Refuge.

Strategies:
1. Conduct biweekly waterfowl, shorebird and waterbird censuses from September through June and coordinate surveys with the annual inter-agency mid-winter waterfowl survey.

2. Continue monitoring of existing heron and egret rookeries and annually survey suitable riparian areas for new colonies (See Strategy 1.B.2).

3. Pursue opportunities to recruit qualified volunteers and develop partnerships with resource agencies, academic institutions and private organizations to accomplish monitoring and research projects related to Refuge habitats and wildlife.

4. Develop and annually update a list of Refuge monitoring needs with universities in the region and other agencies which conduct research.

5. Develop surveys on the South Stone Lake, Headquarters, and Wetland Preserve Units and other lands as they come under Refuge management.

6. Develop data management strategies to store data and make data available to other researchers.

7. Assess feasibility of creating tricolored blackbird habitat in grassland habitat (e.g., planting large California blackberry patches and expanding tule areas in wetlands for nesting).

Goal 3. Provide visitors with wildlife-dependent recreation, interpretation and education opportunities which foster an understanding of the Refuge's unique wildlife and plant communities in an urban setting.

Objective 3.A: Within the next five years, recruit and maintain sufficient short and long term volunteers to accomplish three habitat restoration projects, eight wildlife surveys, six environmental education programs, and remain active in offering a variety of other volunteer opportunities.

Rationale: Refuge volunteer programs are a vital instrument for providing educational and interpretive opportunities to the public and for assisting with biological monitoring and visitor use programs. The reauthorization of the National Wildlife Refuge Volunteer and Community Partnership Enhancement Act of 1998 illustrates the importance of volunteer programs and community partnerships in helping to fulfill the mission of the National Wildlife Refuge System.

Strategies:
1. Broaden the scope of volunteer tasks and define volunteer positions to better utilize the diverse interests, talents and abilities of residents in the surrounding communities.
2. Develop a Refuge volunteer manual to aid the volunteer coordinator with planning and implementing the volunteer program.
3. Provide at least one comprehensive volunteer training opportunity per year with a revised and updated volunteer training manual and other educational opportunities.
4. Develop and maintain a volunteer database.
5. Pursue opportunities to collaborate on expanding volunteer activities with the Sacramento Regional County Sanitation District, Cosumnes River Preserve and Delta Meadows State Park.
6. Recruit Student Conservation Association, AmeriCorps, California Conservation Corps and other interns to

work in a variety of programs.
7. Explore and continue ongoing outreach efforts to recruit quality volunteers.
8. Expand opportunities for specific one-time volunteer events, ongoing individual opportunities and ongoing group opportunities, including community service hour use opportunities.
9. Continue and expand volunteer participation in three habitat restoration projects on the Headquarters Unit, including 176 acres of managed and passive seasonal and permanent wetlands, 82 acres of wet meadow and upland native grasslands and 83 acres of riparian habitats.
10. Maintain and expand volunteer participation in eight ongoing wildlife monitoring surveys including waterbird monitoring, nest box monitoring, rookery surveys, landbird mistnetting/disease monitoring, sandhill crane surveys, grasslands monitoring, frog malformation survey and Swainson's hawk/burrowing survey.
11. Maintain and expand volunteer participation in six environmental education programs including school groups, special group tours, partnering with schools on curricula, special events, volunteer work and teacher workshops.

Objective 3.B: Construct adequate facilities and develop programs for visitors to visit the Refuge seven days a week to observe, photograph and enjoy the Refuge's unique natural habitats and wildlife during all seasons of the year with a target of 10,500 visit opportunities per year by 2009.

Rationale: Wildlife observation and photography are two of the six priority visitor uses identified in the National Wildlife Refuge System Improvement Act of 1997. These wildlife dependent activities were identified in the EIS (USFWS 1992) and should be offered on the Refuge. Currently, the Refuge has limited visitor access to two days per month and, as a result, the expectations of the visiting public are not being met A great potential also exists to provide visitors opportunities for wildlife observation and photography from boats. To prevent disturbance of wildlife, boats would be limited to using trolling motors. A no-wake zone on the entire Refuge would minimize conflicts with other users, water quality degradation, erosion to levees and disturbance to wildlife. Boating would be allowed from June to September to minimize impacts to heron rookeries and Swainson's hawks nesting along riparian corridors.

Strategies:

1. Construct two photography blinds on the Headquarters and North Stone Lake units.
2. Construct restrooms on the Beach Lake, Headquarters and South Stone Lake units.
3. Construct two miles of universally accessible trails and 200 feet of boardwalk on the Headquarters Unit.
4. Construct a safe entrance road and parking area for approximately 40 vehicles on the Headquarters Unit
5. Construct a viewing platform on the Headquarters Unit overlooking newly constructed wetlands.
6. Construct a safe vehicular access point, a parking area for 15 cars and a trail and a wildlife observation platform on the southern portion of the North Stone Lake Unit, accessible from Hood-Franklin Road. Design and locate facilities to minimize impact on sandhill cranes, arctic nesting geese, giant garter snakes and burrowing owls.
7. Provide parking for up to 20 cars at the boat launch on the South Stone Lake unit to provide wildlife viewing, photography, fishing and associated cartop boating opportunities. Only non-motorized or electric motor-only boats would be allowed on South Stone Lake from June through September. South Stone Lake would be an enforced no-wake zone.
8. Construct 1.5 miles of foot trails and 200 feet of boardwalk on the South Stone Lake unit open to the public seven days a week with seasonal restrictions.
9. Develop a boat-accessible haul-out site, walking trail and viewing blind on the South Stone Lake Unit (i.e., Lodi Peninsula)..
10. Provide parking and boat launch capacity for a maximum of 10 cartop boats (including canoes and kayaks) on

Wildlife observation and photography are two of the six priority public uses identified in the National Wildlife Refuge System Improvement Act of 1997.
Photo by USFWS

the Beach Lake unit at the end of Elliott Ranch Road to provide wildlife viewing, photography and fishing opportunities for pre-registered groups in SP Cut from June through September.

11. Once visitor use facilities are made available on the Headquarters unit, shift the focus of the Beach and North Stone Lake units within one year from open-touring days to pre-registered school and docent-guided tour groups.
12. Develop guided tours for the Wetland Preserve Unit.
13. Restrict land-based visitor use near habitat suitable for heron/egret rookeries, nesting Swainson's hawks and other areas used by nesting migratory birds during sensitive laying and incubation periods (approximately February to June 15).
14. Minimize disturbance to sandhill crane foraging and roosting habitats on the Refuge by restricting public access during October through March.
15. Reduce potential spread of invasive species by visitors by restricting access to paved or graveled trails and maintaining trails in good condition through regular weed control.

Objective 3.C: Within five years, develop an environmental education program with a target of providing 80 opportunities per year for groups with an outdoor experience where visitors become aware of the Refuge's role in the conservation of Central Valley and Sacramento San Joaquin Delta habitats and their fish and wildlife.

Rationale: Environmental education is one of the six priority visitor uses identified in the National Wildlife Refuge System Improvement Act of 1997. The Refuge provides a unique opportunity for the local community to experience Central Valley habitats and wildlife in proximity to an urban area. Refuge-based environmental educational activities can also be integrated into both indoor and outdoor classroom curriculums.

Strategies:
1. Offer up to four staff and/or docent lead environmental education tours on the Refuge per week.
2. Within five years, conduct teacher workshops to develop an environmental education program featuring teacher lead tours with a target of training six to 12 groups of teachers per year.
3. Develop a Junior Biologist Trail as part of the proposed Blue Heron Trail System on the Headquarters Unit to be used by schools and other groups and individuals.
4. Develop a Refuge elementary school curriculum manual for teachers to use while visiting the Refuge that includes pre- and post-visitation activities.
5. Explore feasibility of a Refuge fee area to support environmental education programs and general maintenance of visitor use areas.

Objective 3.D: Within five years, develop two interpretive programs where visitors could learn of the Refuge's role in conserving the Central Valley and Sacramento-San Joaquin Delta habitats and their fish and wildlife, with an emphasis on outdoor hands-on experiences.

Rationale: Interpretation is one of the six priority visitor uses identified in the National Wildlife Refuge System Improvement Act of 1997. Interpretive activities can introduce the public to the Refuge's habitat management activities and familiarize them with the conservation efforts that protect local natural resources.

Strategies:
1. Develop a self-guided trail as part of the proposed Blue Heron Trails System on the Headquarters Unit with hands-on learning stations within two years.
2. Develop a class/group staging area and 5 open air interpretive shelters with one kiosk and exhibits as part of the Blue Heron Trails system that would accommodate approximately 40 children at a time.
3. Develop interpretive displays on the Headquarters Unit that illustrate

traditional dwellings, various subsistence strategies and the overall lifestyle of local American Indian Tribes (see Objective 4.F).

4. Continue existing guided hikes and offer one additional interpretive docent guided hike per month.

5. Develop interpretive panels and exhibits on South Stone Lake Unit.

6. Develop self-guided trail and interpretive displays for the Wetland Preserve Unit.

7. Develop a variety of written interpretive materials such as brochures, flyers and handouts

Objective 3.E: Within five years, the Refuge will provide safe, boat-only fishing with day use parking facilities to accommodate a maximum of 20 boats on South Stone Lake and a minimum of ten boats on SP Cut from June through September.

Rationale: Fishing is one of the six priority visitor uses identified in the National Wildlife Refuge System Improvement Act of 1997. Fishing has traditionally occurred on South Stone Lake and surrounding Delta waterways since American Indians occupied the area. In this objective, "safe," is defined as the absence of any fishing-related safety incidents.

Strategies:
1. Develop and maintain a safe public parking lot and boat launch facilities to accommodate a maximum of 20 cartop (not trailered) boats on the South Stone Lake unit, including an informational kiosk with maps and brochures on regulations, health warnings, species identification and Refuge boundaries. Boating will extend up the SP Cut to the culvert on the South Stone Lake unit.

2. Provide a launch for pre-registered canoe/kayak groups in SP Cut on the Beach Lake unit from June through September. Access would be from the end of Elliott Ranch Road and a no wake zone will be enforced.

3. Fishing will be in accordance with all State regulations. Fishing will not include take of frogs or crayfish and will only be done with rod and reel.

4. Restrict water-based visitor use near habitat suitable for heron/egret rookeries and Swainson's hawks during sensitive laying and incubation periods (approximately February to June 15).

5. Develop facilities for mobility impaired persons to enter and exit canoes and kayaks safely.

6. See objective 3.B for other strategies related to opportunities for boating programs.

Objective 3.F: Continue to expand the Refuge outreach program, targeting the local community and nontraditional users, by expanding partnerships for the annual Walk on the Wildside event and prepare for a minimum of four appropriate off-Refuge events, per year, to increase awareness of the Refuge's role in conserving Central Valley and Sacramento San Joaquin Delta habitats and their associated fish and wildlife.

Rationale: Environmental education is one of the six priority visitor uses identified in the National Wildlife Refuge System Improvement Act of 1997. The urban location of the Refuge provides opportunities for the Service to educate broader audiences within the local community, including nontraditional users, about the Refuge's role in conserving Central Valley habitats and wildlife and the benefits the Refuge provides to the surrounding communities and Central Valley.

Strategies:
1. Maintain Refuge website for a one-stop source of information about Refuge history, events and biological resources with links to the Stone Lakes National Wildlife Refuge Association and other partners.

2. Continue and expand partnerships for the annual Walk on the Wildside festival to celebrate the National Wildlife Refuge System and other events, such as International Migratory Bird Day.

3. Participate in at least four appropriate local off-refuge events each year, such

as the Lodi Crane Festival and Salmon Festival.

4. Support the Stone Lakes National Wildlife Refuge Association by actively participating in their events, activities and meetings and making monthly contributions to Association outreach related materials, including newsletters, the website and brochures.

5. Collaborate with and assist local resource-oriented agencies and city departments, such as the Elk Grove Community Service District, on outreach programs involving the Refuge.

6. Develop new portable refuge displays for use at fairs, shows and festivals.

7. Expand the number of presentations given to schools, conservation groups and public service organizations.

Goal 4. In cooperation with tribal representatives, identify and protect cultural resources on the Refuge and educate the public regarding American Indians and the history of the region.

Objective 4.A: Prepare a cultural resources overview of the Refuge, within 15 years of CCP approval.

Rationale: Although record searches have been conducted for all Service-managed properties, a complete compilation of site records and relevant reports summarizing the number and locations of all recorded sites within the approved Refuge boundary would aid in planning land conservation, management and landowner outreach. Refuge planning efforts would be enhanced by identifying the location and composition of collections of human remains, funerary objects, sacred objects, or objects of cultural patrimony that were discovered and removed from within the approved Refuge boundary prior to the Service assuming land management authority. However, this overview would be for the sole purpose of identifying cultural resources and these collections would not fall under Service jurisdiction.

Strategies:
1. Compile and maintain all existing baseline data on cultural resources sites, surveys and reports within one mile of the approved Refuge boundary.

2. In consultation with archaeologists and tribal representatives, approximate the location of unrecorded sites and culturally sensitive areas within the approved Refuge boundary by using site records, maps and other data.   Identify cultural resources issues and needs and draft potential solutions.

3. To aid with Refuge planning, identify the location and composition of any collections of human remains and Native American Grave Protection and Repatriation Act (NAGPRA) covered items removed from within the approved Refuge boundary prior to the Service's assumption of land management.

Objective 4.B: Within 15 years of CCP approval, evaluate conditions of known cultural resource sites on Refuge managed lands and conduct seasonal monitoring of known sites.

Rationale: The Service is required to ensure that the integrity of any cultural sites on Refuge lands are protected. As a result of the activities of previous landowners, sites may have been impacted or may still be vulnerable to continued degradation (e.g.,erosion, traffic, theft). Therefore, sites should be evaluated by qualified professionals and measures to stop and/or reverse deterioration of the sites should be developed and implemented.

Strategies:
1. Conduct monthly monitoring visits of known cultural resource sites on the North Stone Lake Unit to ensure that existing grazing protection measures are intact.

2. As needed, consult with professional archaeologists, local tribal representatives and the Regional Office Archaeologist regarding any necessary protection or remediation measures for cultural resource sites.

3. Develop additional measures to protect sites and/or remediate past damages, if necessary.

Objective 4.C: *Identify and delineate any cultural resources on new lands coming under Refuge management.*

Rationale: Identifying historic properties on lands as they come under Refuge management will enable staff to ensure that any restoration and management programs for fish and wildlife will also protect the integrity of sensitive cultural resources.

Strategies:
1. As funding is available, a qualified archeologist will survey new properties coming under Refuge management to locate and delineate, as needed, any known or previously unrecorded cultural resource sites.
2. In consultation with the appropriate Service or other professional cultural resource experts, evaluate sites on newly-managed properties to identify any protection, restoration, and/or management measures that may be necessary.

Objective 4.D: *Meet annually with the Ione Band of Miwok Indians and other concerned tribal groups to discuss land management and restoration activities planned for the upcoming field season.*

Rationale: The Service has agreed to meet annually with the Ione Band of Miwok Indians to keep them informed regarding planned Refuge activities. Meetings will also provide a forum for tribal representatives to present any of their proposals or discuss other concerns that relate to management of Refuge lands.

Strategies:
1. As the Service has previously agreed, hold an annual meeting to review previous projects or summarize management or restoration projects and public events that are planned by the Refuge for the upcoming year, whether or not these activities will require formal State Historic Preservation Office consultation.
2. Review and reissue, if appropriate, any special use permits for traditional activities such as plant collecting for basket weaving.

Objective 4.E: *Within five years, begin developing a memorandum of understanding or agreement with the Ione Band of Miwok Indians or with other involved tribal organizations to facilitate compliance with the Native American Grave Protection and Repatriation Act (NAGPRA) and to establish protocols for treating human remains and associated funerary objects, sacred objects or objects of cultural patrimony.*

Rationale: Due to previous land uses, some Refuge lands and other properties within the approved Refuge boundary have human remains or NAGPRA covered items exposed on the surface of the ground. Currently, the Refuge consults with the Ione Band of Miwok Indians regarding land management programs and the status of burial sites. In addition to the Ione Band, other organizations may need to be consulted. In consultation with the Ione Band and other relevant authorities and experts, the Refuge has implemented some protection measures and assisted with some repatriation of human remains and funerary items. Since more sites are expected to come under Refuge management and to facilitate compliance with NAGPRA, a formal agreement with tribal groups should be developed to define the protocol to be followed when protection, repatriation and re-interment measures are appropriate.

Strategies:
1. Develop an agreement that includes the following elements: notification procedures; when appropriate, procedures for collection of human remains and associated funerary objects, sacred objects, or objects of cultural patrimony; criteria for defining NAGPRA covered items; any data collection or study of materials that may be warranted; guidelines for any

temporary or permanent curation of non-repatriated materials; and a re-interment protocol.

Objective 4.F: Develop a minimum of two interpretive panels and exhibits, located various on units, to educate the public regarding the cultural resources of the Refuge and past and present American Indian cultural practices, within 15 years of CCP approval.

Rationale: Developing interpretive and educational materials to increase public understanding about local American Indian peoples is necessary, given the abundance of cultural resources within the approved Refuge boundary and the historic role of Indians in the Sacramento-San Joaquin Delta. These materials will aid Refuge staff in explaining historical ecological conditions, the importance of restoring and/or maintaining the integrity of those conditions and the role fish and wildlife played in American Indian culture and history.

Strategies:
1. Develop exhibits for the Headquarters and Beach Lake units to illustrate traditional dwellings, various subsistence strategies and the overall lifestyle of local American Indian peoples.
2. Solicit input and advice from concerned tribal representatives in planning, information gathering and review of educational, interpretive and outreach programs and publications. Work with Tribes and universities to identify the messages and resources that would be most appropriate to share with the public.
3. In publications or exhibits, provide a brief history of the indigenous peoples of greater California, scaling down to the Sacramento Valley and then to the Sacramento-San Joaquin Delta region to educate the public.
4. Include a cultural resource element in special events held on the Refuge.

6 Implementation and Monitoring

Once the preferred management alternative and CCP are finalized and approved and the Service has notified the public of its decision, the implementation phase of the CCP process begins. Implementation occurs over a period of 15 years, during which the CCP will serve as the primary reference document for all Refuge planning, operations and management until it is formally revised. The Service will implement the final CCP with assistance from existing and new partner agencies and organizations and from the public.

The activities required to realize the management goals discussed in this CCP are referred to as "projects" below. Every effort will be made to implement the projects by the established deadlines. However, the implementation timing of the management activities proposed in this document is contingent upon a variety of factors, including:
- Completion of detailed step-down management plans
- Funding
- Staffing
- Compliance with other Federal laws and regulations
- Partnerships
- The results of monitoring and evaluation

Each of these factors is described briefly below as they apply to the Service's proposed action.

Step-Down Management Plans

Some projects or types of projects require more in-depth planning than the CCP process is designed to provide. For these projects, the Service prepares step-down management plans. In essence, step-down management plans provide the additional planning details necessary to implement

management strategies identified in a CCP. Refuge staff members have already completed a number of step-down plans. These include fire management, grazing, land protection and mosquito integrated pest management plans. This CCP proposes several new step-down plans that are identified in Table 2, along with target dates for completion.

Funding and Staffing

Resources are required to adequately operate any national wildlife refuge including initial capital outlay for equipment, facilities, labor and other expenses as well as recurring, annual costs for staff, contracts, supplies, maintenance and other recurring expenses (See Table 3, Estimated Initial Capital Outlay to Implement CCP). The estimated initial capital outlay for the Refuge, described in this CCP would cost approximately $10 million. Not all of these capital expenditures would occur in the same year as many of these expenses would be most likely implemented over the course of several years. The detailed descriptions of objectives and their associated implementation strategies serve as a guide to the ideal time frame in which to implement capital expenditures. The largest costs for initial outlays are for visitor

Table 2. Step-down Management Plans

Step Down Plan	Target for Completion
Fisheries Management Plan	2008
Invasive Weed - Integrated Pest Management Plan	2008
Volunteer Plan	2009
Comprehensive Inventory and Monitoring Plan	2009
Habitat Management Plan	2009

services and habitat restoration as should be expected for an urban refuge.

To fully implement this CCP, personnel dedicated to the Refuge would include:
• 1 Project Leader
• 1 Deputy Project Leader
• 1 Wildlife Biologist
• 1 Administrative Support Assistant
• 1 Outdoor Recreation Specialist
• 1 Park Ranger
• 1 Motor Vehicle Operator
• 1 Engineering Equipment Operator

Annual contracts or cooperative agreements will also be needed to provide specialized services beyond the core Refuge functions, for which staff are required. The recurring staffing and other costs associated with CCP implementation total approximately six hundred and seventy thousand dollars (See Table 4, Estimated Annual Cost to Implement the CCP). This is approximately a 54 percent increase over the Fiscal Year 2006 operations budget of 435,000.

Compliance Requirements

This CCP was developed to comply with all Federal laws, executive orders and legislative acts to the extent possible. Some activities , particularly those that involve revising an existing step-down management plan or preparing a new one, would need to comply with other laws or regulations. In addition to NEPA and the Improvement Act, full implementation of all components of this CCP would require compliance with:
• Executive Order 11988 (Floodplain Management)
• Executive Order 12372 (Intergovernmental Review of Federal Programs)
• Executive Order 11593 (Protection of Historical, Archaeological, and Scientific Properties)
• Executive Order 11990 (Protection of Wetlands)
• Executive Order 12996 (Management and General Public Use of the National Wildlife Refuge System)
• Executive Order 12898 (Environmental Justice in Minority Populations and Low-Income Populations)

• Secretarial Order 3127 (Hazardous Substances Determinations)
• Endangered Species Act of 1973, as amended
• Refuge Recreation Act of 1962, as amended
• National Historic Preservation Act of 1966, as amended

Partnership Opportunities

As described in Chapter 1, a wide array of private and public partners play an important role in helping the Service achieve its goals and objectives for the Refuge. The Service will continue to rely on these and other partners in the future to help implement the final CCP and to provide input for future CCP updates. This draft CCP identifies many projects that provide new opportunities for existing or new partners. There is great potential for more public participation and assistance in the management and interpretation of the Refuges. The Service welcomes and encourages more public participation in the Refuges.

Adaptive Management

This draft CCP provides for adaptive management of the Refuge. Adaptive management is a flexible approach to long-term management of biotic resources that is directed by the results of ongoing monitoring activities and new data. Management techniques, objectives and strategies are regularly evaluated in light of monitoring results, new scientific understanding and other new information. These periodic evaluations are used to adapt management objectives and techniques to better achieve the Refuge's goals. Monitoring is an essential component of adaptive management in general and of this draft CCP. Specific monitoring strategies have been integrated into the goals and objectives whenever possible.

Plan Amendment and Revision

Refuge CCPs are meant to evolve with each individual Refuge unit. The Improvement Act specifically requires that CCPs be formally revised and updated at least every 15 years. The formal revision process will follow the same steps as the CCP process (see Chapter 2: The Planning Process). In the meantime, the Service will annually review a checklist of the goals, objectives and management strategies of this CCP to assist in tracking and evaluating progress. The final CCP would also be informally reviewed by Refuge staff while preparing annual work plans and updating the Refuge database. It may also be reviewed during routine inspections or programmatic evaluations. Results of any or all of these reviews may indicate a need to modify the plan. The goals described in the final CCP would not change until they are re-evaluated as part of the formal CCP revision process. The objectives and strategies, however, may be revised to address changing circumstances or to take advantage of increased knowledge of the resources on the Refuge. If changes are required, the level of public involvement and associated NEPA documentation would be determined by the Refuge Manager, in accordance with Service policy.

Table 3. Estimated Initial Capital Outlay to Implement the CCP

Expenditure (Related Strategy)	Unit Cost	Unit	Quantity	Total Cost
Plant trees with beaver exclusion fences (1.A.1)	$15,000	mile	1.3	$19,500
Expand riparian zone at S. Stone Lakes and HQ (1.A.2)	$6,000	acre	5	$30,000
Restore 20 acres by HQ to native plants (1.A.3)	$8,000	acres	20	$160,000
Enhance sub-canopy in BL, NSL units (1.A.4)	$3,000	acre	115	$345,000
Establish native plant nursery by HQ (1.A.5)	$65,399	ea	1	$65,399
Plant early/mid-seccessional vegetation on west portion of Lewis and SSL Units (1.A.6)	$6,000	acre	126	$756,000
Maintain/expand fencing along SP cut (1.B.3)	$10,000	mile	1.3	$13,000
Modify existing water delivery system on SSL Unit (1.C.1)	$25,000	mod.	1	$25,000
Map elodea at SSL and initiate control (1.G.3)	$10,000			$10,000
Enhance burrowing owl habitat at NSL unit (1.H.4)	$15,000	exp. unit	1	$15,000
Establish experimental native grass plots (1.J.1)	$8,000	acre	0.25	$2,000
Restore Lewis Unit grasslands (1.J.5)	$8,000	acre	108	$864,000
Develop a levee and flood control channel maintenance MOU (1.M.4)	$20,000	program dev.	1	$20,000
Develop a Refuge volunteer manual (3.A.2)	$19,505	ea	1	$19,505
Develop a Refuge volunteer database (3.A.4)	$19,505	ea	1	$19,505
Construct photography blinds (3.B.1)	$15,000	ea	2	$30,000
Construct restrooms at BL, SSL and HQ (3.B.2)	$50,000	ea	3	$150,000
Construct 2 miles of universally accessible trails at HQ Unit (3.B.3)	$100,000	mile	2	$200,000
Construct 200 ft. boardwalk at HQ (3.B.3)	$1,060	feet	200	$212,000
Construct entrance road and parking area (3.B.4)	$1,500,000	ea	1	$1,500,000
Construct viewing platform and associated boardwalk on HQ site (3.B.5)	$500,000	ea	1	$500,000
Construct parking lot, trail and observation platform at NSL site (3.B.6)	$620,000	ea	1	$620,000
Improve entrance road and parking area at SSL boat launch site (3.B.7)	$1,000,000	ea	1	$1,000,000
Construct foot trails at SSL (3.B.8)	$100,000	mile	1.5	$150,000
Construct 200 ft. boardwalk at SSL (3.B.8)	$1,060	feet	200	$212,000
Develop boat haul out and assoc. trail at Lodi Gun Club (3.B.9)	$30,000	ea	1	$30,000
Improve parking at BLU Lewis tract at end of Elliott Ranch Road (3.B.10)	$163,000	ea	1	$163,000
Develop a Junior Biologist Trail at HQ complete with entrance signs, universally accessible trails, entrance kiosk, interpretive panels (3.C.3, 3.D.1)	$1,630,000	ea	1	$1,630,000
Develop a an EE elementary school curriculum (3.C.4)	$19,505	ea	1	$19,505
Develop open air shelters (5) and main shelter (3.D.2)	$50,000	ea	6	$300,000
Develop local Indian displays at HQ (3.D.3, 4.F.)	$50,000	ea	1	$50,000
Develop interpretative panels at SSL (3.D.5)	$50,000	ea	1	$50,000
Develop self-guided trail and interpretative displays for the Wetlands Preserve Unit (3.D.6)	$300,000	ea	1	$300,000
Develop written interpretative materials (3.D.7)	$19,505	ea	1	$19,505

Table 3. (continued)

Expenditure (Related Strategy)	Unit Cost	Unit	Quantity	Total Cost
Develop parking lot and boat launch at SSL (3.E.1)	$55,000	ea	1	$55,000
Develop disabled accessible boating facilities (3.E.5)	$50,000	ea	1	$50,000
Compile baseline cultural resources data (4.A.1)	$5,000	ea	1	$5,000
Locate unrecorded cultural sites and sensitive areas (4.A.2)	$5,000	ea	1	$5,000
Identify location of human remains and NAGPRA items located in collections and museums (4.A.3)	$5,000	ea	1	$5,000
Develop exhibits for the HQ and BL units to illustrate traditional dwellings, subsistence strategies and lifestyle (4.F.1)	$25,000	ea	2	$50,000
Total				**$9,669,919**

Table 4. Estimated Annual Cost to Implement the CCP

Expenditure (Related Objective)	Unit Cost	Unit	Quantity	Total Cost
Staff Salaries and Benefits (# indicates position filled)				
# Refuge Refuge Manager/PL - GS-13	$102,450	ea	1	$102,450
# Refuge Assistant Refuge Manager - GS -12	$84,032	ea	1	$84,032
Wildlife Biologist GS-9	$65,680	ea	1	$65,680
# Administrative Support Assistant - GS-7	$54,268	ea	1	$54,268
# Outdoor Recreation Planner GS-11	$70,122	ea	1	$70,122
Park Ranger GS-7	$47,372	ea	1	$47,372
Engineering Equipment Operator - WG - 8	$53,560	ea	1	$53,560
# Motor Vehicle Operator WG - 6	$46,540	ea	1	$46,540
Maintenance supplies (1.D., 1.H., 1.F.)	$50,000	1	1	$50,000
Invasive weed management program (1.A., 1.B., 1.D., 1.E., 1.F., 1.H.)	$60,000	ea	1	$60,000
Water/pumping cost (1.I., 2.A.)	$20,000	ea	1	$20,000
Maintain 40-60 acres or agricultural fields (2.A.5)	$5,000	ea	1	$5,000
Levee and flood control channel maintenance MOU coordination (1.M.4)	$10,000	ea	1	$10,000
Water quality monitoring (1.N.)	$60,000	ea	1	$60,000
Travel/training	$6,000	ea	1	$6,000
Supplies	$25,000	ea	1	$25,000
Printing	$5,000	ea	1	$5,000
Pump-out for restroom	$5,000	ea	1	$5,000
Total				**$667,574**

References

Ahl, J. S. B. 1991. Factors affecting contributions of the tadpole shrimp, *Lepidurus packardi*, to its oversummering egg reserves. Hydrobiologia 212:137-143.

Air Resources Board of California (ARB). 2006. ARB Health-Related Factsheets.
http://www.arb.ca.gov/research/health/fs/fs.htm
Viewed on June 29, 2006.

American Community Survey (ACS). 2004. 2004 American Community Survey Fact Sheet. Sacramento County, California.
http://factfinder.census.gov
Viewed on June 20, 2006.

Aquatic Nuisance Species Taskforce (ANSTF). 2003. National Management Plan for the Genus Eriocheir (Mitten Crabs). Prepared by the Chinese Mitten Crab Working Group, November 2003.
http://www.anstaskforce.gov/control.php

Bennyhoff, J.A. 1977. Ethnogeography of the Plains Miwok. Center for Archaeological Research at the University of California at Davis. Publication 5.

Bloom, P.H. 1980. The status of the Swainson's hawk in California, 1979. U.S. Department of Interior, Bureau of Land Management, Sacramento. Project W-54-R-12, Job II-8, Final Rep. 42pp.

California Agricultural Statistics Service (CASS). 2004. Summary of County Agricultural Commissioner's Reports, 2002-2003. California Agricultural Statistics Service, Sacramento, CA.

California Department of Food and Agriculture (CDFA). 2006. Pest Ratings of Noxious Weed Species and Noxious Weed Seed. State of California Department of Food and Agriculture, Division of Plant Health and Pest Prevention Services.
http://www.cdfa.ca.gov.
Viewed on June 20, 2006.

California Department of Fish and Game (DFG). 2000. The status of rare, threatened, and endangered animals and plants of California, Annual Report for 2000. California Department of Fish and Game. Sacramento, CA. 226 pp.

California Department of Fish and Game (DFG). 2001. The status of rare, threatened, and endangered animals and plants of California, Annual Report for 2000. California Department of Fish and Game. Sacramento, CA. 226 pp.

California Department of Fish and Game (DFG). 2004. California Natural Diversity Database Rarefind.

California Department of Fish and Game (DFG). 2006. California Wildlife: Conservation Challenges (California's Wildlife Action Plan). Prepared by Bunn, David, Andrea Mummert, Roxie Anderson, Kirsten Gilardi, Marc Hoshovsky, Sandra Shanks and Kiffanie Stahle. Wildlife Health Center, University of California, Davis.

California Department of Water Resources (DWR). 2006. Where Rivers Meet...the Sacramento-San Joaquin Delta. State Water Project. http://www.publicaffairs.water.ca.gov/swp/delta.cfm Viewed on June 27, 2006.

California Labor Market Information (CLMI). 2006. http://www.labormarketinfo.edd.ca.gov Viewed on June 20, 2006.

California Partners in Flight (CPIF). 2000. Version 1.0. The Draft Grassland Bird Conservation Plan: a Strategy for Protecting and Managing Grassland Habitats and Associated Birds in California (B. Allen, lead author). Point Reyes Bird Observatory, Stinson Beach, CA. http://www.prbo.org/CPIF/Consplan.html Viewed on June 27, 2006.

California Regional Water Quality Control Board – Central Valley Region (CRWQCB-CVR). 2004. The Water Quality Control Plan (Basin Plan) for the California Regional Water Quality Control Board Central Valley Region. http://www.swrcb.ca.gov/rwqcb5/available_documents/index.html#anchor616381 Viewed on July 25, 2006.

California Regional Water Quality Control Board – Central Valley Region (CRWQCB-CVR). 2006. ORDER NO. R5-2006-0054: Individual Discharger Conditional Waiver of Waste Discharge Requirements for Discharges from Irrigated Lands.

Central Valley Joint Venture (CVJV). 1990. Central Valley Habitat Joint Venture Implementation Plan, A Component of the North American Waterfowl Management Plan.

City of Elk Grove (CEG). 2000. East Franklin Specific Plan. http://www.egplanning.org/projects/eastfranklin_sp/index.html Viewed on July 21, 2006.

City of Elk Grove (CEG). 2006. Community Profile, Residential. http://www.elkgrovecity.org/economic-development/ Viewed on June 26, 2006.

Cogswell, H.L. 1977. Water birds of California. University of California Press, Berkeley. 399pp.

Eckert, A.W. and K.E. Karalus. 1981. The wading birds of North America. Doubleday and Co., Garden City, NY. 252 pp.

Executive Order 13112. 1999. Invasive Species. Federal Register vol. 64, No. 25. February 8, 1999.

Fitch, H.S. 1941. The feeding habits of California garter snakes. California Department of Fish and Game 27:1-32.

Garrett, K. and J. Dunn. 1981. Birds of southern California. Los Angeles Audubon Society 408pp

Grinnell, J. and A.H. Miller. 1944. The distribution of the birds of California. Pacific Coast Avifauna No. 27, 608 pp.

Hart, J.A. 1999. Draft North Stone Lake Restoration and Management Master Plan. HART Inc. 82 pp.

Heady, H. F. 1977. Valley grassland. Pages 491-514 In M. G. Barbour and J. Major, eds. Terrestrial vegetation of California. John Wiley and Sons, New York.

Heady, H. A. 1988. Valley grassland. Pages 491–514. M. G. Barbour and J. Major, editors. Terrestrial vegetation of California. Wiley Interscience, John Wiley and Sons, New York, New York, USA.

Helm, B. 1998. The biogeography of eight large branchiopods endemic to California. Pages 124–139 in C. W. Witham, E. Bauder, D. Belk, W. Ferren, and R. Ornduff (eds.), Ecology, conservation, and management of vernal pool ecosystems – proceedings from a 1996 conference. Sacramento, CA: California Native Plant Society.

Ivey, G.L. and C.P. Herziger. 2001. Distribution of greater sandhill crane pairs in California 2000. California Department of Fish and Game. Sacramento, California.

James, A.H. 1977. Sandhill cranes breeding in Sierra Valley, California. West Birds 8:159-160.

Jones and Stokes Associates, Inc. 1989. Urban Forest Master Plan for the Buffer Lands Surrounding the Sacramento Regional Wastewater Treatment Plant. (JSA 88-078.) Sacramento, CA. Prepared for County of Sacramento, Department of Public Works, Sacramento, CA.

Jones, Roger, B. Young, and T. Faith. 1994. 1992 - 1994. Summary of Bufferlands Fish Sampling Program 1992-1994.

Johnsgard, P.A. 1975a. North American game birds of upland and shoreline. University of Nebraska Press, Lincoln. 183 pp.

Katibah, E.F. 1984. A brief history of riparian forests in the Central Valley of California in California Riparian Systems: Ecology, Conservation, and Productive Management. Edited by R.E. Warner and K.M. Hendrix. University of California Press, California. Pages 23-29.

Kroeber, A.L. 1932. The Patwin and Their Neighbors. University of California Publications I American Archaeology and Ethnology 29 (4):254:-23.

Kuminoff, Nicolai V., Alvin D. Sokolow, Ray Coppock, George E. Goodman, Greg Poseley and Susan Kester. 2000. Agriculture in the Sacramento Region: Trends and Prospects. Materials and summary from the forum: The Future of Agriculture in the Sacramento Region held February 14, 2000.

Littlefield, C. D., and G. L. Ivey. 2002. Washington State Recovery Plan for the Sandhill Crane. Washington Department of Fish and Wildlife, Olympia, Washington. 71 pages.

McCaskie, G., P. De Benedictis, R. Erickson, and J. Morlan. 1979. Birds of northern California, an annotated field list. 2nd ed. Golden Gate Audubon Society, Berkeley. 84 pp.

Merriam, C.H. 1907. Distribution and Classification of the Mewan Stock of California. American Antiquity n.s. 9:338-357.

National Wildlife Refuge Association (NWRA). 2002. Silent Invasion. National Wildlife Refuge Association. Washington D.C.

Pacific Flyway Council. 1997. Pacific Flyway management plan fro the Central Valley Population of Greater Sandhill Cranes, Pacific Flyway Comm. [c/o Pacific Flyway Representative USFWS], Portland, OR 97232. Unpubl. Rept. 44 pp. + appendices.

Polite, C. 2000. Swainson's Hawk (*Buteo swainsoni*), California's Wildlife Volume II: Birds, Report B121 (Updates from Zeiner, D.C., W.F. Laudenslayer, Jr., and M. White, Eds., 1988-1990), California Department of Fish and Game, Sacramento.

Remsen, J.V., Jr. 1978. Bird species of special concern in California. Calif. Dept. of Fish and Game, Sacramento. Wildl. Manage. Admin. Rep. No. 78-1. 54 pp.

Riparian Habitat Joint Venture (RHJV). 2004. Version 2.0. The Riparian Bird Conservation Plan: a Strategy for Reversing the Decline of Riparian Associated Birds in California. California Partners
in Flight. http://www.prbo.org/calpif/pdfs/riparian.v-2.pdf.
Viewed on June 26, 2006.

Robins, J.D., and J.E. Vollmar. 2002. Livestock grazing and vernal pools from Wildlife and Rare Plant Ecology of Eastern Merced County's Vernal Pool Grasslands, IN: Wildlife and Rare Plant Ecology of Eastern Merced County's Vernal Pool Grasslands. Merced County Natural Community Conservation Plan and Habitat Conservation Plan. http://www.mercedncccp-hcp.net/vollmar/
Viewed on June 26, 2006.

Rossman, D.A., N.B. Ford, and R.A. Siegel. 1996. The garter snakes: evolution and ecology. University of Oklahoma Press, Norman. 332 pp.

Sacramento Area Council of Governments (SACOG). 2001. Documentation: Projections for Population, Housing, Employment and Primary/Secondary Students.

Sacramento County (Sacramento County). 2000. Environmental Impact Report - East Franklin Specific Plan and Associated Rezones and Subdivisions Maps Known as Jungkeit Dairy, Laguna Creek South, Franklin Meadows, Laguna Meadows, and JAS Development. Volume 1 of 3.

Sacramento County Department of Agriculture (Sacramento County). 1999. Agricultural crop and livestock report. 1999. Sacramento, CA.

Sacramento County Department of Agriculture (Sacramento County). 2002. Agricultural crop and livestock report. 2002. Sacramento, CA.

Sacramento County Division of Public Health (Sacramento County). 2006. 2005 Summary
of West Nile Virus Activity in Sacramento County.
http://www.sacdhhs.com/article.asp?ContentID=1402
Viewed on July 21, 2006.

Sacramento Forecast Project (SFP). 2006. Sacramento County Economic Forecast.
http://www.csus.edu/indiv/j/jensena/sfp/sa11/sac5/sac/sacramen.htm#C
Viewed on June 20, 2006.

San Francisco Estuary Project (SFEP). 2000. State of the Estuary 2000, Restoration
Primer. S.F. Estuary Project, Oakland, CA.

Smithsonian Zoological Park. 2006. Western Riparian Systems: Magnets for Migrants.
Written by John Sterling http://nationalzoo.si.edu/ConservationAndScience/
MigratoryBirds/Fact_Sheets/default.cfm?fxsht=5
Viewed on August 11, 2006.

Stebbins, G. Ledyard. 1965. Colonizing species of the native California flora. In The Genetics
of Colonizing Species, Academic Press, NY, pp. 173-191.

Terres, J.K. 1980. The Audubon Society encyclopedia of North American birds. A. Knopf,
New York. 1100 pp.

Thomas, Carmen. 1997. Contaminant Concentrations in Water, Sediment, and Biota from
Stone Lakes National Wildlife Refuge. U.S. Fish and Wildlife Service, Environmental
Contaminants Division, Sacramento Fish and Wildlife Office. 34 pp.

Thomas, C.M., and T.C. Maurer. 2003. Toxicity of Stormwater Runoff at Stone Lakes
National Wildlife Refuge, 1999-2000, Final Report, Investigation No.: 199910003, U.S.
Department of the Interior, Fish and Wildlife Service, Portland, Oregon.

Tremaine, K.J. 1997. Revisiting Archaeological Sites CA-SAC-85 and 86 within the Stone
Lakes National Wildlife Refuge, Sacramento County, California. June 1997. U.S. Fish
and Wildlife Service Document. 83 pp.

U.S. Army Corps of Engineers. 1987. Morrison Creek Stream Group, California – Beach-
Stone Lakes Reconnaissance Report. Sacramento, CA.

U.S. Census Bureau (USCB). 2000. Census 2000 Redistricting Data (Public Law 94-171)
Summary File.
http://factfinder.census.gov
Viewed on June 20, 2006.

U.S. Census Bureau (USCB). 2006. State and County Quick Facts, Sacramento County,
California.
http://quickfacts.census.gov
Viewed on June 20, 2006.

U.S. Department of Commerce (USDOC). 2006. U.S. Census Bureau News: Released 12:01
a.m. (EDT), June 21, 2006.

U.S. Environmental Protection Agency (USEPA). 2006. Green Book Non-Attainment Areas.
http://epa.gov/air/oaqps/greenbk/index.html
Viewed on June 29, 2006.

U.S. Fish and Wildlife Service (USFWS). 1992. Environmental impact statement with appendices for Stone Lakes National Wildlife Refuge Project, Sacramento County, California; Final. With technical assistance provided by Jones & Stokes Associates, Inc. (JSA 91-047.) Sacramento, CA.

U.S. Fish and Wildlife Service (USFWS). 1993. Determination of threatened status for the giant garter snake. Federal Register 58(201):54053-66.

U.S. Fish and Wildlife Service (USFWS). 1994. 50 CFR Part 17. Endangered and Threatened Wildlife and Plants; Determination of Endangered Status for the Conservancy Fairy Shrimp, Longhorn Fairy Shrimp, and the Vernal Pool Tadpole Shrimp; and Threatened Status for the Vernal Pool Fairy Shrimp. Federal Register Notice Vol. 59 Number 180. September 19, 1994.

U.S. Fish and Wildlife Service (USFWS). 2003a. Stone Lakes National Wildlife Refuge Bird List. May 2003.

U.S. Fish and Wildlife Service (USFWS). 2003b. Stone Lakes Contaminant Assessment Process Final Report. Service Database. 19 February 2003b

U.S. Fish and Wildlife Service (USFWS). 2003c. 50 CFR Part 17. Plants; Final Designation of Critical Habitat for Four Vernal Pool Crustaceans and Eleven Vernal Pool Plants in California and Southern Oregon; Final Rule. Federal Register Notice Vol. 68 Number 151. Aug 6, 2003.

U.S. Fish and Wildlife Service (USFWS). 2003d. Toxicity of Stormwater Runoff at Stone Lakes National Wildlife Refuge, 1999-2000, Final Report, Investigation No.: 199910003. July 2003.

U.S. Fish and Wildlife Service (USFWS). 2004. Monitoring and Reporting Program Plan: San Luis National Wildlife Refuge Complex. Environmental Contaminants Division, Sacramento Fish and Wildlife Office, Sacramento, CA.

U.S. Fish and Wildlife Service (USFWS). 2006. Recovery Plan for Vernal Pool Ecosystems of California and Southern Oregon. Sacramento, CA.
http://www.fws.gov/sacramento/es/recovery_plans/vp_recovery_plan_links.htm
Viewed on June 26, 2006.

Vanicek, C. David. 1992. Memorandum, Dec 2, 1999 to Tom Harvey.

Wylie 1997. Biological Resources Division (BRD) survey for the giant garter snake.

Personal Communications

Geupel, Geoff. Point Reyes Bird Observatory (PRBO). 2003.

Ivey, Gary. Private Consultant. 2003.

Marty, J. 2004. Biological Resources Division (BRD). Science Talk, September 2004.

Treiterer, Beatrix. U.S. Fish and Wildlife Service (USFWS). September 2004, July 2006.

www.ingramcontent.com/pod-product-compliance
Lightning Source LLC
Chambersburg PA
CBHW081222280526
45787CB00006B/2490